Church Year

Series A
Lent • Easter • Ascension • Pentecost

Study Guide

By Donald R. Schiemann
and William Ney
Edited by Thomas J. Doyle

CPH™

SAINT LOUIS

Assistant to the editor: Cynthia Anderson

Write to the Library for the Blind, 1333 S. Kirkwood Road, St. Louis, MO 63122-7295 to obtain this study in braille or large print for the visually impaired.

Liturgical materials are from *Lutheran Worship,* copyright © 1982 by Concordia Publishing House. All rights reserved.

Scripture taken from the HOLY BIBLE: NEW INTERNATIONAL VERSON®. NIV®. Copyright © 1973, 1978, 1984 by the International Bible Society. Used by permission of Zondervan Publishing House. All rights reserved.

Copyright © 1995 Concordia Publishing House
3558 South Jefferson Avenue, St. Louis, MO 63118-3968
Manufactured in the United States of America

Contents

Introduction

About the Series

This course is 1 of 12 in the Church Year series. The Bible studies in this series are tied to the 3-year lectionary. These studies give participants the opportunity to explore the Old Testament Lesson (or lesson from the book of Acts during the Easter season), the Epistle Lesson, and the Gospel Lesson appointed for each Sunday of the church year. Also, optional studies give participants the opportunity to study in-depth the lessons appointed for festivals that fall on days other than Sunday (e.g., Ascension, Reformation, Christmas, Christmas Eve, Maundy Thursday, Good Friday, Epiphany).

Book 1 for years A, B, and C in the lectionary series will include 17 studies for the Scripture lessons appointed for the Sundays and festival days in Advent, Christmas, and Epiphany. Book 2 will include 17 studies for the lessons appointed for the Sundays and festival days in Lent and Easter and of lessons appointed for Ascension and Pentecost. Book 3 (15 sessions) and book 4 (16 sessions) for years A, B, and C will include studies that focus on the lessons appointed for the Pentecost season.

After a brief review and textual study of the Scripture lessons appointed for a Sunday or festival day, each study is designed to help participants draw conclusions about each of the lessons, compare and contrast the lessons, discover a unifying theme in the lessons (if possible), and apply the theme to their lives. At the end of each study, the Scripture lessons for the next Sunday and/or festival day are assigned for participants to read in preparation for the next study. The Leaders Guide for each course provides additional information on appointed lessons, answers to the questions in the Study Guide, a suggested process for teaching the study, and devotional or worship activities tied to the theme.

May the Holy Spirit richly bless you as you study God's Word!

Session 1

The First Sunday in Lent

Genesis 2:7–9, 15–17, 3:1–7; Romans 5:12–19;
Matthew 4:1–11

Focus

Theme: *Tempting, Isn't It?*

Law/Gospel Focus

Each of us has one or more areas where we find ourselves vulnerable to temptation. We struggle to resist, yet we give in more often than we care to admit. Christ resisted temptation, and in His righteousness we find forgiveness, hope, and strength to live as God's people.

Objectives

As we study the Word today, we pray that God, by His Spirit, will lead us to
1. recognize our weaknesses and our vulnerability to Satan's lies and temptations;
2. repent for the times we have willingly entered into temptation;
3. confess Jesus Christ as the one whom God has sent on our behalf to overcome sin, death, and the devil;
4. rejoice that through the obedience of Christ we have been made righteous.

Opening Worship

Pray the following responsive prayer:

Leader: Since Satan's power is still great, and we are an easy mark for his assaults,

Participants: we implore You, Lord, to give us the strength to resist him.

Leader:	Strengthen our will and graciously enable our hearts to do Your will.
Participants:	Send us Your Holy Spirit to empower our hearts with the desire and joy to resist the old nature within us.
Leader:	As we observe the power of Satan rampant in our world, causing many to worship him as You would be worshiped,
Participants:	we implore You to curb his power and bring to naught his distressing activity among us.
Leader:	We give You humble thanks that as our substitute Your Son Jesus Christ successfully overcame the devil.
Participants:	Grant us such success so that our days upon the earth may be peaceful and joyful.
Leader:	In the name of Him who conquered the forces of evil for us,
Participants:	even our Lord Jesus Christ, we earnestly pray. Amen.

(Adapted from *Prayers Responsively* by Theodore Bornhoeft. Concordia Publishing House © 1984. All rights reserved.)

Introduction

A pastor asked his confirmation class if they could be tempted with things like liver, turnips, squash, spinach, or prunes. A corporate "Ugh!" arose from the class. He then asked about ice-cream sundaes, chocolate-chip cookies, chocolate bars, and the like. The class readily admitted that he had found their weak spots.

Greek mythology tells the story of Achilles, the hero of the Trojan war, who as a child was dipped in the waters of the river Styx. His mother, Thetis, wanted to make him invulnerable. The result of that plunge was that every spot of Achilles' body, except for his heel, was safe against wounds. For many years Achilles escaped unhurt, but at last a poisoned arrow from the bow of the Trojan Paris found the weak spot—Achilles' heel—and inflicted a mortal blow.

So Satan tempts Christians where they are the weakest. He identifies our "Achilles' heel" and works to break down our resistance and our resolve. Money, desire, popularity, and prestige—the devil attacks God's people in moments of weakness and leads them to despair.

1. Think of famous people who fell into disrepute because they surrendered to temptation. How might they have rationalized their behavior? How were they particularly vulnerable?

2. Think of people in the Bible who yielded to temptation (Genesis 3:4 and John 8:44). How were their lives affected? How were their relationships affected?

3. An entire society may have certain weaknesses that lead to a broad acceptance and practice of sin. How have our particular weaknesses affected our North American society?

Inform

Read the following summaries of the Scripture lessons for the First Sunday in Lent.

Genesis 2:7–9, 15–17; 3:1–7—God the Creator forms Adam and provides everything he needs to live in a perfect world. He also gives Adam the freedom to choose obedience to his loving Creator. Obedience meant life in the presence of God. Disobedience meant separation and death. Satan enters the Garden of Eden and tempts our first parents with the ultimate temptation, "You will be like God." After giving in to the temptation, Adam and Eve are filled with shame and make coverings for themselves.

Romans 5:12–19—God created humankind in His own image. Adam lost that image when he sinned and could only pass on to his descendants the wages of his sin. God in His grace, however, sent His

Son as the second Adam and by His perfect obedience and righteousness, Jesus paid the penalty for our sin. God declares us forgiven and righteous, for Jesus' sake.

Matthew 4:1–11—As the anointed Savior, at His Baptism, Jesus begins His ministry in the wilderness, tempted by Satan. The King who came to redeem lost and condemned sinners and bring them into His kingdom (Titus 2:14; 1 Peter 2:9) is offered a kingdom without the cross. Standing firm on God's Word, Jesus resists the devil's temptations and embarks upon His mission to save the world from sin, death, and destruction.

1. Though Adam and Eve had everything in the Garden of Eden they still sinned. Why did Adam and Eve give in to temptation?

2. Adam and Eve knew what was right and wrong from the beginning. God had put His Word in their hearts (Romans 2:14–15) and had set His will before them concerning the tree of the knowledge of good and evil. Satan tells Eve, however, that God is holding out on her. "You will be like God, knowing good and evil" (Genesis 3:5). Why was this such a temptation to Eve? Is it still a temptation today? Explain.

3. When Eve was first confronted by Satan, how did she resist his temptation? How did Satan respond?

4. Read Genesis 5:1–3 and Romans 5:12. What was the effect of the fall into sin on all people?

5. Sin so permeated humankind that death reigned "even over those who did not sin by breaking a command" (Romans 5:14). Psalm 51:3–5 describes the sin we commit and the sin we inherit. In order to rescue us from the power of sin, what were the necessary qualifications for our Savior?

6. In Matthew 4:1–11, how is Jesus described? How did Satan use these things to tempt Jesus?

7. When Jesus was confronted by Satan, how did He withstand temptation? How did Satan respond? What was Jesus' continued response? What does this teach us about dealing with temptation?

8. Why was it so important for Jesus to resist temptation? Reread Romans 5:17–19.

Connect

1. In the Lord's Prayer we pray, "And lead us not into temptation." Martin Luther wrote the following explanation of this petition: "God tempts no one. We pray in this petition that God would guard and keep us so that the devil, the world, and our sinful nature may not deceive us or mislead us into false belief, despair, and other great shame and vice. Although we are attacked by these things, we pray that we may finally overcome them and win

the victory." According to this explanation, from where do we receive the strength for overcoming temptation?

2. How can we deal effectively with our weaknesses? How does the fact that we have a perfect Savior help us? Read Romans 6:2–3, 11–14.

3. Martin Luther referred to one of the "ancient fathers" when he wrote: "Not the approach of temptations, but our entertaining them and yielding to them we can prevent. You cannot prevent the birds from flying over your head, but you can prevent them from building their nests in your hair." How? Read 1 Peter 5:8–9.

4. In our struggle with the devil, the world, and our own sinful self we sometimes find ourselves on the losing side. Ultimately, the final victory is ours in Jesus Christ. Read 1 John 2:1–2. Is this passage license or comfort? Why would this passage provide significant comfort to someone who has just given in to temptation?

Vision

During This Week

1. Make a list of those areas in your life where you are easily tempted. Seek God's help to avoid places and situations where these temptations are most likely to arise.

2. Write down or memorize passages of Scripture that will be particularly helpful to you when you are confronted with temptation. (E.g., 1 Corinthians 6:19–20; Romans 6:22; and Romans 8:2.)

Closing Worship

Pray or sing together "Fight the Good Fight" (*LW* 299).

> Fight the good fight with all your might;
> Christ is your strength, and Christ your right.
> Lay hold on life, and it shall be
> Your joy and crown eternally.
>
> Run the straight race through God's good grace;
> Lift up your eyes, and seek His face.
> Life with its way before us lies;
> Christ is the path, and Christ the prize.
>
> Cast care aside, lean on your guide;
> His boundless mercy will provide.
> Trust, and enduring faith shall prove
> Christ is your life and Christ your love.
>
> Faint not nor fear, His arms are near;
> He changes not who holds you dear;
> Only believe, and you will see
> That Christ is all eternally.

Scripture Lessons for Next Sunday

Read in preparation for the Second Sunday of Lent Genesis 12:1–8; Romans 4:1–5, 13–17; and John 4:5–42.

Session 2

The Second Sunday in Lent

Genesis 12:1–8; Romans 4:1–5, 13–17;
John 4:5–26 (27–30, 39–42)

Focus

Theme: *Empty, Filled, Spilled*

Law/Gospel Focus

Apart from God, the lives of all people are spiritually empty. People fool themselves into thinking that they can fill the emptiness with the things of this world. Only God fills that emptiness with the gift of His Son, our Savior.

Objectives

As we immerse ourselves in the Word today, by the working of the Holy Spirit in the Word, we will

1. identify the spiritual emptiness in which we were born;
2. confess the tendency to fill our lives with the things of this world to mask our spiritual hunger;
3. affirm Jesus as the one who fills that need, and express the purpose, meaning, and value that God gives in a life of service and witness.

Opening Worship

Read responsively this adaptation of the Collect for the Second Sunday in Lent:

Leader: As we gather today we have deliberately put ourselves in the way of the Word.

Participants: We come into the presence of the Word and have God's promise that it will take root.

All: O God, whose glory it is always to have mercy, be gracious to all who have gone astray from Your ways, and bring them again with penitent hearts and steadfast faith to embrace and hold fast the unchangeable truth of Your Word; through Jesus Christ, Your Son, our Lord, who lives and reigns with You and the Holy Spirit, one God, now and forever. Amen.

Introduction

People need the Lord. Greg Nelson and Phill McHugh described that need in a song they wrote:

> "Ev'ry day they pass me by, I can see it in their eye;
> Empty people filled with care, headed who knows where.
> On they go through private pain, living fear to fear.
> Laughter hides the silent cries only Jesus hears."
>
> (© 1983 River Oaks Music Company/Shepherd's Fold Music. Admin. by EMI Christian Music Publishing. All rights reserved. Reprinted by permission.)

Many people lead what the world tells them are "full" lives. They have wealth, health, and looks. Their friends all share the same pursuit for material things. Yet inside they are empty. They know that they hurt, fear, and need, but they cannot understand why all their accumulations don't fill the void in their hearts.

At one time or another, most of us have experienced the same sense of hurt, fear, and need. We may have been devastated by a great loss. Maybe we did or said something we immediately regretted, and we realized that there was no going back. At these times, we try to convince ourselves and others that we can "handle it." And we try to fill the emptiness with something that will enable us to go on.

1. What did all of the following people have in common: Judy Garland, Elvis Presley, John Belushi, Marilyn Monroe, Jimi Hendrix, Janis Joplin? How did people perceive them in life? How were they perceived after their death?

2. Some fill their lives with material things, while others search for spiritual fulfillment. For all the new religious movements in our world today, so many people remain empty and alone. Why?

3. Apart from God, people fill their lives with things that result in hopelessness. What does it mean to be fulfilled? See Romans 15:13.

Inform

Read the following summaries of the three lessons for this Second Sunday in Lent.

Genesis 12:1–8—God calls Abram to a new life. Abram travels with his family and possessions to the Promised Land. God promises to bless Abram and to bless the whole world through his "offspring," the Messiah. Abram responds in worship and thanksgiving to his gracious God. The plan of salvation unfolds.

Romans 4:1–5, 13–17—Abraham's life is an example of God's pure grace. In mercy God called Abraham to be "the father of many nations" (4:18) and Abraham believed God's Word. Abraham did not work to earn God's love and forgiveness. Rather, it was a gift from God. Salvation is *never* a reward or payment for our efforts. Like Abraham, we believe God declares us "not guilty" because of His great love in Jesus Christ, the promised offspring and Savior of the world.

John 4:5–42—Jesus welcomes sinners! The woman at the well had three strikes against her: she was Samaritan, she had had five husbands, and she was living in an adulterous relationship. Her life was empty, and she went from relationship to relationship in a vain attempt to find meaning and acceptance. In the eyes of her contemporaries, she was truly a sinner. Yet in Jesus, she finds God's unconditional love and forgiveness. The Savior promised in the Sacred Scriptures offers her "living water" for life eternal.

The Samaritan woman, whose spiritual life had long ago dried up, was filled with the "springs of water." Jesus found her and called her to be an heir of the promise. More than that, her faith overflowed to others as she shared the good news about Jesus. Abraham's faith spilled over into a life of obedience; the Samaritan woman's faith spilled over into a life of joy and of sharing the good news of the Savior.

1. List the seven promises God makes in His covenant with Abraham (Genesis 12:2–3).

2. As God calls Abram to faith, He gives purpose and meaning to life. By the power of God's grace, Abraham becomes a blessing to others. Describe this "spillover effect." See Genesis 22:17–18; 26:4; and Acts 3:25.

3. God promises Abraham a life filled with blessings through the coming Savior. These blessings, however, are not only to Abraham, but also to his descendants. Who are these descendants? See Romans 4:16–17.

4. A gas tank filled with water is still, for all practical purposes, an empty tank. The Samaritan woman, whose life was filled with passion and pleasure, was still an empty person. What did Jesus offer to her? What did He mean? See John 4:13–14.

5. What do the following passages say about "water" and God's purpose?
   • Jeremiah 2:13

- John 7:37–39

- Revelation 7:17

6. In what ways is Baptism "living water?" See Romans 6:4 and 1 Peter 3:21.

═══ **Connect** ═══

1. Imagine! What would your life look like today if you had never known Jesus Christ?

2. How has Jesus filled your life? What blessings have you experienced through faith in Him?

3. The following passages are examples of the "spillover effect" of our new life in Christ. Describe the effect in each passage.
    - Esther 9:22

    - John 13:34–35

    - 1 Peter 1:22

4. Our Christian faith and life are never "private and confidential." We live in relation to God, to people, to our congregation, and to

the world. List some specific areas where, by word and deed, your life of faith will touch the lives of others.

Vision

During This Week

1. Are there any particular "problem sins" that rob you of living your Christian life to the fullest? Ask the Lord's forgiveness for these sins and, by the power of His grace, seek to live your life to the glory of God.
2. At the beginning of each day this week, write down the name of a person whose life you can touch in some way as you live your "filled life." Pray that God will give you the opportunity in some way to share Christ's love with that person.

Closing Worship

Read together Psalm 72.

> Endow the king with Your justice, O God,
>> the royal son with Your righteousness.
> He will judge Your people in righteousness,
>> Your afflicted ones with justice.
> The mountains will bring prosperity to the people,
>> the hills the fruit of righteousness.
> He will defend the afflicted among the people
>> and save the children of the needy;
>> he will crush the oppressor.
>
> He will endure as long as the sun,
>> as long as the moon, through all generations.
> He will be like rain falling on a mown field,
>> like showers watering the earth.
> In his days the righteous will flourish;
>> prosperity will abound till the moon is no more.
> He will rule from sea to sea
>> and from the River to the ends of the earth.

The desert tribes will bow before him
       and his enemies will lick the dust.
The kings of Tarshish and of distant shores
       will bring tribute to him;
the kings of Sheba and Seba
       will present him gifts.
All kings will bow down to him
       and all nations will serve him.

For he will deliver the needy who cry out,
       the afflicted who have no one to help.
He will take pity on the weak and the needy
       and save the needy from death.
He will rescue them from oppression and violence,
       for precious is their blood in his sight.

Long may he live!
       May gold from Sheba be given him.
May people ever pray for him
       and bless him all day long.
Let grain abound throughout the land;
       on the tops of the hills may it sway.
Let its fruit flourish like Lebanon;
       let it thrive like the grass of the field.
May his name endure forever;
       may it continue as long as the sun.
All nations will be blessed through him,
       and they will call him blessed.

Praise be to the LORD God, the God of Israel,
       who alone does marvelous deeds.
Praise be to His glorious name forever;
       may the whole earth be filled with His glory.
Amen and Amen.

Scripture Lessons for Next Sunday

Read in preparation for the Third Sunday in Lent Isaiah 42:14–21; Ephesians 5:8–14; and John 9:13–17, 34–39.

Session 3

The Third Sunday in Lent

Isaiah 42:14–21; Ephesians 5:8–14; John 9:13–17, 34–39

Focus

Theme: *Speak Up!*

Law/Gospel Focus

It is so easy to talk about the doom and gloom we hear and read about in the news. Christians are too often silent in word and deed about the greatest news of their lives and of history. Jesus forgives us our failures and empowers us to speak up.

Objectives

As we read God's Word, by His Spirit at work in the Word, we will see that
1. God has acted in a mighty way to redeem people, and He wants the message to be told;
2. By the power of the Gospel, God moves people past their timidity toward bolder witness of the saving message of Jesus;
3. God has made us His people so that we may "declare the praises of Him who called you out of darkness into His wonderful light" (1 Peter 2:9).

Opening Worship

Pray together the responsive prayer.

Leader: May Your Holy Spirit enlighten us to the mysteries of Your Word.

Participants: Give us clear insight that we may confidently lead others into Your light.

Leader: Bless our efforts to enlighten the world with the truth of Your Gospel, and keep the light of faith burning brightly in our hearts.

Participants: Use us to alleviate the sufferings of the sick and
make us guides to the blind.

All: Amen.

Introduction

Would you share the Gospel with a crowd of 300 young men in leather jackets?

In 1993, a Canadian youth singing group traveled to Lviv, a city in Ukraine, to share the Gospel through song. They were invited to sing at a veterinary school. When they arrived, they saw that the majority of their audience (over 350 people) was young men in leather jackets. This was certainly a threatening sight by our western standards. Would the men listen as the youth explained the Gospel message of their songs through their translators? Would the crowd make fun of the group? Would this be a "wasted concert?"

1. The black leather jacket is one of the many cultural images that might elicit fear in some. What other images or situations make us reluctant to share our faith?

2. When it comes to sharing our faith, we all have doubts and fears. It seems true that people, by nature, are hostile toward a Christian witness. What reasons can you suggest for those feelings of hostility? What overcame that hostility in you? Read Romans 1:16 and 1 Peter 1:23.

3. God has a heart for the lost. What comfort is that to us as we share our faith? Read Ezekiel 18:21–23.

Inform

Read through the following summaries of the Scripture lessons for the Third Sunday in Lent.

Isaiah 42:14–21—God cannot keep silent. He has done great things, all of them leading to the fulfillment of the Gospel promise of Genesis 3:15 and other Messianic prophecies. The effect of the fulfillment of these prophecies will be so dramatic that darkness will become light and rough places will become smooth. As wondrous as this message is, there are still those who pay no attention and hear nothing.

Ephesians 5:8–14—Live as children of the light. A life in the light will be markedly different from a life lived in total darkness. Christ has redeemed us and, through faith, we are His own. All facets of life are new and different now. Christ, the light of the world, shines on us with His grace and mercy to enable us to walk and to talk as children of the Light.

John 9:13–17, 34–39—Jesus gives sight to a man born blind, who now confesses, "I see!" On one level, the man refers to Jesus' miraculous healing. On the spiritual level, the man acknowledges Jesus as Savior. Jesus reveals Himself as the Son of Man—God's promised Deliverer for His people. With his "eyes" truly opened, the man responds in gratitude and worship: "Lord, I believe."

1. Isaiah 42:15–16 is a powerful announcement of God's great activity on earth. The first display (v. 15) is the spectacular events in nature. Why are the things listed in verse 16 of even greater wonder and importance?

2. God's forgiveness, life, and salvation are offered freely in the Gospel. Through the gift of faith, we receive these wonderful gifts. Our confession of faith speaks of *who* we are and whose we are. Read Acts 4:12; 10:43; and Romans 10:13. What do these verses tell us about our confidence in Christ?

23

3. What assurance did the blind man receive from Jesus? What did he believe about Jesus?

4. Many people choose their own gods in life. Some say, "It doesn't matter what god you confess, as long as you are sincere." Others say that all roads—or all gods—lead to the same place. What does God say in Isaiah 42:17? What does this mean for those who say, "All religions are the same?"

5. Sin, unbelief, hypocrisy, and false religion are as prevalent today as they were in Bible times. What is the Christian's response to these things according to Ephesians 5:11? What does Paul mean by "Wake up, O sleeper, rise from the dead" (v. 14)?

6. In last week's study, we read about the Samaritan woman at the well. What did she have in common with the man born blind in today's Gospel? Read John 4:39–42 and 9:27–34.

Connect

1. What kind of an audience did the Samaritan woman and the man born blind have? Humanly speaking, what audience would have been easier to speak to? Knowing what actually happened, discuss the implications of Ephesians 5:14 for your life.

2. Recall the story of the Canadian youth group and the "leather jacket crowd." "Humanly speaking," describe what could have happened.

3. Speaking from a "heavenly perspective," what could have happened?

4. Listen as the leader reads the account of what actually happened.
5. Think about situations where you failed to speak up about your faith. What *could* have happened if you *had* shared?

6. Botched opportunities, fear of failure or scorn, and bad experiences have often led people to be silent about their Savior. When witnessing and evangelism are discussed, people often feel guilty about their silence and at the same time feel helpless to do anything to change. We need to hear God's Word of grace and power. Read responsively 1 John 2:12–14.

Leader: I write you, dear children,
Participants: because your sins have been forgiven on account of His name.
Leader: I write to you, fathers,
Participants: because you have known Him who is from the beginning.
Leader: I write to you, young men,
Participants: because you have overcome the evil one.
Leader: I write to you, dear children,
Participants: because you have known the Father.
Leader: I write to you, fathers,
Participants: because you have known Him who is from the beginning.
Leader: I write to you, young men,
Participants: because you are strong, and the Word of God lives in you, and you have overcome the evil one.

Vision

During This Week

1. Our family can be a safe place to begin sharing our faith with other Christians. Seek opportunities this week to share with your family what Christ means to you.
2. As you become more comfortable talking about Jesus with other Christians, ask the Lord to provide you with an opportunity to speak to non-Christians.
3. Always commend the results of your witness to our Lord.

Closing Worship

Pray together Psalm 71:1–8.

> In You, O Lord, I have taken refuge;
>   let me never be put to shame.
> Rescue me and deliver me in Your righteousness;
>   turn Your ear to me and save me.
> Be my rock of refuge,
>   to which I can always go;
> give the command to save me,
>   for You are my rock and my fortress.
> Deliver me, O my God, from the hand of the wicked,
>   from the grasp of evil and cruel men.
>
> For You have been my hope, O Sovereign Lord,
>   my confidence since my youth.
> From birth I have relied on You;
>   You brought me forth from my mother's womb.
>   I will ever praise You.
> I have become like a portent to many,
>   but You are my strong refuge.
> My mouth is filled with Your praise,
>   declaring Your splendor all day long.

Scripture Lessons for Next Sunday

Read in preparation for the Fourth Sunday in Lent Hosea 5:15–6:2; Romans 8:1–10; and Matthew 20:17–28.

Session 4

The Fourth Sunday in Lent

Hosea 5:15–6:2; Romans 8:1–10; Matthew 20:17–28

Focus

Theme: *Cross, Crowns, and Servants*

Law/Gospel Focus

Our sinful nature often seeks self-glorification based on what we think is our own goodness. It is more comfortable to see ourselves deserving a crown than a cross. Jesus went to the cross for us so that we might have the crown of everlasting life. By the power of the message of the cross, we are led to receive our crown as a gift and to find greatness by being God's servants.

Objectives

By the working of the Holy Spirit through the Word of God, we will be led to

1. repent for smug self-righteousness in our dealings with God and with others;
2. confide in what God has done for us through His Son Jesus Christ to make things right with Him;
3. wear the crown as Christ did—as a servant—so that through our words and actions we might glorify God.

Opening Worship

Pray the following litany:
Leader: Remember, O Lord, our congregation, Your people,
Participants: who are nothing without You,
Leader: who need the Word of Your forgiveness,
Participants: who need comfort and solace,
Leader: who need healing and help,
Participants: who need courage and strength,

Leader: who need counsel and guidance,
Participants: who need food and shelter,
Leader: who need correction and admonition,
Participants: who need acceptance and assurance,
Leader: who need zeal and a willing mind,
Participants: who need example and direction,
Leader: who need charity and goodness,
Participants: who need humility and honesty,
Leader: who need liberty and peace,
Participants: who need wisdom and insight,
Leader: who need faith and hope,
Participants: who need love and joy,
All: for we are Your people gathered by Your Spirit around Word and sacraments, that we may be scattered to share Your love through Christ, our Lord. Amen.

Introduction

What does it cost to become an Olympic athlete? People see the gold medalists and envision themselves on the podium. They don't take into account the blood, sweat, and tears that are the price for the victory. Parents know this feeling all too well. Who gets the bill for raising a child? If the child becomes famous, do his or her parents become famous as well? Can you name the parents of any of the United States Presidents or the Prime Ministers of Canada? Ultimately, parents get the bill while children get the glory.

1. Read Isaiah 53:4–6 and 2 Corinthians 5:21. "Jesus got the bill, we got the glory." What is meant by this statement?

2. What would move God to enter this kind of an arrangement? Read Deuteronomy 7:7–8.

3. The New Testament speaks of three different kinds of love: physical love, friendship love, and sacrificial love. How would you describe the type of love about which we have just read?

4. A man bought the rusted remains of an old Rolls Royce for $50. He lovingly restored the vehicle, putting much time, effort, and money into the project. Twenty-five years after he bought the car, in its reconditioned state it was worth $25,000. Relate this story to what God has done for you. What value do you have?

Inform

Look at the brief summaries of the Scripture lessons for the Fourth Sunday in Lent.

Hosea 5:15–6:2—In spite of their sin, God does not turn His back on people. He is pictured here waiting patiently for Israel to repent. He has the power to restore repentant sinners so that they might "live in His presence."

Romans 8:1–10—In Christ, there is no condemnation. He has paid the price for all of our sins, and we are no longer bound by the law of sin and death. Our old sinful self owned nothing but death. The mind controlled by the Spirit is "life and peace." Having been liberated from the power of sin through faith in Christ Jesus, we are now free to serve the living God.

Matthew 20:17–28—Jesus directs our attention to the cross and the empty tomb. These had to happen that we might be bought back from the power of sin and death. As redeemed people our glory is in serving Him who gave His life as a ransom.

1. What words or phrases in Hosea 6:1–2 indicate what God will do for sinners?

2. With Hosea 6:1–2, we move from the picture of God as the Judge who sentences the guilty to God as the Physician who heals the wounded. It is a transition from justice to mercy and grace. Read again Romans 8:1–2. What or who makes this transition possible?

3. Read Romans 8:1–2 and Matthew 20:18–19. How does Jesus' death and resurrection lead to "no condemnation" for believers?

4. Read Mark 10:35–37. James and John joined their mother in making a bold request. What did they ask of Jesus? How does their attitude reflect the world's priorities?

5. Contrast the request of James and John with Paul's attitude in Galatians 6:14.

6. Read Revelation 2:10. What does it mean to be "faithful"?

Connect

1. In John Milton's *Paradise Lost*, Satan says, "It is better to reign in hell than to serve in heaven." No one, it seems, prefers humility to honor. From our study today, what are the true joys of serving our Lord? Use personal examples if you wish.

2. Read Hosea 5:15–6:2 and 1 John 1:9 again. What can we do about past failures? How can we "shake loose" from selfish attitudes and habits?

3. In the list below, check which relationships in your life could be changed for the better through the power of the cross.
   ❑ Relationship with spouse
   ❑ Relationship with employer
   ❑ Relationship with parents
   ❑ Relationship with children
   ❑ Relationship with neighbors
   ❑ Relationship with church
   ❑ Relationship with friends
   ❑ Relationship with teacher
   ❑ Others:

4. In the Lord's Prayer, we are reminded that as forgiven people, we will forgive others ("Forgive us our trespasses as we forgive those who trespass against us"). In this light, how might the relationships in question 3 change as Christ is brought into the situation?

Vision

During This Week

1. As a servant of Jesus, pray that the Lord can use you in a way that will bring Him special honor this week.
2. If a relationship with a friend or family member has been strained, bring Christ into that situation and, if possible, share the outcome with the class next week.
3. Think about servant activities you or the class can do.

Closing Worship

Read together Psalm 34:1–10.

I will extol the LORD at all times;
> His praise will always be on my lips.
My soul will boast in the LORD;
> let the afflicted hear and rejoice.
Glorify the LORD with me;
> let us exalt His name together.
I sought the LORD, and He answered me;
> He delivered me from all my fears.
Those who look to Him are radiant;
> their faces are never covered with shame.
This poor man called, and the LORD heard him;
> He saved him out of all his troubles.
The angel of the LORD encamps around those who fear Him,
> and He delivers them.
Taste and see that the LORD is good;
> blessed is the man who takes refuge in Him.
Fear the LORD, you His saints,
> for those who fear Him lack nothing.
The lions may grow weak and hungry,
> but those who seek the LORD lack no good thing.

Scripture Lessons for Next Week

Read in preparation for the Fifth Sunday in Lent Ezekiel 37:1–3, (4–10), 11–14; Romans 8:11–19; and John 11:47–53.

Session 5

The Fifth Sunday in Lent

Ezekiel 37:1–3, (4–10), 11–14; Romans 8:11–19;
John 11:47–53

Focus

Theme: *One Nation under God*

Law/Gospel Focus

Our world is separated from God and made up of people who are separated from one another. In Christ, we are united in one nation—His church—where He gives us a new identity. We are His people. We belong to Him and, as Christians, we belong to each other.

Objectives

God is at work in His Word. As we study His Word, the Holy Spirit will lead us to
  1. see how sin drives us apart from God and each other;
  2. repent for our self-serving sin, which has built walls between us and God and others;
  3. depend upon Jesus alone to restore us;
  4. rejoice in our membership in the family of God;
  5. serve our Lord in work and witness to bring others to Christ that they, too, might know the joy of belonging to Him.

Opening Worship

Pray or sing together the hymn "Blest Be the Tie That Binds" (*LW* 295) and then speak the litany that follows.

> Blest be the tie that binds
> Our hearts in Christian love;
> The unity of heart and mind
> Is like to that above.

Before our Father's throne
We pour our ardent prayers;
Our fears, our hopes, our aims are one,
Our comforts and our cares.

We share our mutual woes,
Our mutual burdens bear,
And often for each other flows
The sympathizing tear.

From sorrow, toil, and pain
And sin we shall be free,
And perfect love and friendship reign
Through all eternity.

Leader: We come this day, O Lord, as friends to begin and to continue a task.

Participants: We come this day, called into faith in Christ, gathered into His community, enlightened by His Word, sanctified by His Spirit, and kept in faith.

Leader: Lord, in Your mercy remove from us any ill will or troubling spirit that obstructs our mission or restricts our service.

Participants: Teach us to welcome one another; to embrace each other as brothers and sisters in faith; to forgive each other as we have been forgiven; to celebrate with each other, especially in Your presence; to love as we have been loved by You; to care for, help, and support each other and those in need; to be Your people and witnesses to Your love in an alien world.

Leader: Lord, in Your mercy help us to number our days and apply our hearts to wisdom.

Participants: By Your grace, help us to use all that You give to adore, honor, and praise You, our God, Father, Son, and Holy Spirit. Amen.

Introduction

Following World War II, hundreds of thousands of men, women, and children wandered throughout Europe looking for lost friends and families. The political restructuring of Europe combined with the ravages of war left many without home or citizenship. These refugees belonged to no one.

As we draw near to the end of this century, there are more refugees now than at any other time in history. From Cambodia, Vietnam, Cuba, Haiti, Central America, and Eastern Europe, their story is pretty much the same. They have no homes. They belong to no one.

1. In your own words, describe a "spiritual refugee."

2. North America is undergoing a "spiritual revival." People are seeking a spiritual home. They want a sense of spiritual belonging. The New Age religions instruct people on how to search for belonging. They talk about the "journey." Contrast this with Philippians 3:20.

Inform

Read the following brief summaries of the Scripture lessons for the Fifth Sunday in Lent.

Ezekiel 37:1–14—"Can these bones live?" The whitewashed bones symbolized the community of exiles in Babylon. Their hope was completely dead. They were God's people, the bearers of the Messianic promise. They had wandered far from Him, however, and God allowed the Babylonians to conquer their nation and take them into exile. As far as they were concerned, there was no hope. God's Word and promise is so powerful, however, that, as we see in this passage, it can even bring dead bones to life. He can and will restore His people (vv. 12–14).

Romans 8:11–19—The Spirit, who raised Jesus from the dead, dwells also in us. We are counted among the living. As those who are alive in Christ, we belong to God. We are His children and heirs of eternal life in heaven. By His grace, He calls us "sons of God." He claims us as His own. We belong to Him.

John 11:47–53—"The Romans will come and take away both our place and our nation." This was Caiaphas' fear. He had established himself in that which would eventually pass away. Struggling to protect it, he plots the death of Jesus. In the death of Jesus, however, God establishes His kingdom "not only for that nation but also for the scattered children of God, to bring them together and make them one."

1. How is humankind's separation from God manifested in the world? How has this affected you? Have you observed sin and its effects in your nation? In your life? Share some examples.

2. Scan the three texts. What three things does God give to His church to give and sustain life in a dying world? Describe their power.

3. In the Ezekiel passage, the bones are described as being "very dry" (v. 2). Why are they described in this manner?

4. The power of God's Word is depicted in Ezekiel 37:4–6. What is that Word capable of doing?

5. Ezekiel 37:12 points us to the Resurrection. What does Romans 8:11 tell us about the Resurrection?

6. Romans 8:18 speak of our "present sufferings" as being nothing compared to what God has in store for us. As "co-heirs of Christ," to what can we look forward?

7. Caiaphas became an unwitting prophet. The man who seeks the death of Jesus ends up speaking words of life. What words did Caiaphas speak which are special words of comfort to a Christian?

Connect

All of the kingdoms, empires, and nations of history experience a recurring cycle of birth, life, and death. Even the mightiest nation with the greatest resources of people, technology, and military might will one day crumble into the dust of history.

The kingdom of God, however, endures forever. The wonderful thing about this nation is that it is not some kind of exclusive club. On the contrary, it is especially for those who are the least worthy (1 Timothy 1:15).

1. In the hymn "Amazing Grace," John Newton writes, "I once was lost, but now am found." People who have been Christians since their Baptism as infants can be thankful for this wonderful gift. Try and describe, however, what it might be like to have a sense of "lostness." If there is someone in the group who became a Christian recently perhaps they may be willing to share what it means to them to belong to Christ.

2. As a child of God and co-heir with Christ, the Word, Spirit, and Son are at work constantly in your life. Share briefly how they have been at work this past week.

3. During the height of the refugee crisis, groups and individuals were encouraged to sponsor refugees. What would it mean to "sponsor" a spiritual refugee?

4. Trinity Lutheran Church in Republic, Washington, an LCMS congregation, and Christ Lutheran Church in Grand Forks, British Columbia, a congregation of the Lutheran Church—Canada, formed an international dual parish. At a recent joint meeting of the congregations, the comment was made, "Some of us are proud to say 'I'm an American.' Others are proud to say 'I'm a Canadian.' All of us rejoice to confess 'Our citizenship is in heaven!' " List some of the privileges of your heavenly citizenship.

5. For an American to move to Canada, there is a long and involved process to acquire "Landed Immigrant Status." For a Canadian to move to the United States, there is a similar process. Describe the process required to become a citizen of heaven. See Ephesians 2:8–10.

Vision

During This Week

1. Identify a "spiritual refugee" and seek to sponsor that refugee into the kingdom of God.
2. Develop a strategy for sponsoring spiritual refugees into the kingdom in your congregation.
3. Write down the blessings and privileges of citizenship in the kingdom of God and seek ways of sharing this list with others.

Closing Worship

Pray together Psalm 126:1–6.

> When the LORD brought back the captives to Zion,
> we were like men who dreamed.
> Our mouths were filled with laughter,
> our tongues with songs of joy.
> Then it was said among the nations,
> "The LORD has done great things for them."
> The LORD has done great things for us,
> and we are filled with joy.
>
> Restore our fortunes, O LORD,
> like streams in the Negev.
> Those who sow in tears
> will reap with songs of joy.
> He who goes out weeping,
> carrying seed to sow,
> will return with songs of joy,
> carrying sheaves with him.

Scripture Lessons for Next Sunday

Read in preparation for Palm Sunday (Sunday of the Passion) Isaiah 50:4–9b; Philippians 2:5–11; and Matthew 27:11–54.

Session 6

Palm Sunday, The Sunday of the Passion

Isaiah 50:4–9b; Philippians 2:5–11; Matthew 27:11–54

Focus

Theme: *Who for Us and for Our Salvation*

Law/Gospel Focus

In sinful arrogance, we are tempted to "go it alone" in dealing with problems, trying to change sinful habits or attempting to deal with guilt. Invariably, we will find ourselves in greater need than ever. God recognized our greatest need and in His Son did for us what we could never do. He has supplied our greatest needs with the richest measure of His grace.

Objectives

God doesn't leave us in the dark. He speaks clearly to us in His Word, the Bible. As we study His Word today, God grant that we will

1. see how our sin renders us so helpless;
2. be drawn to the one who completely supplies what we need;
3. believe in and live under His all-sufficient grace;
4. rejoice in the new life we receive from our all-sufficient Savior.

Opening Worship

Speak the following litany based on the Epistle Lesson.

Leader: Your attitude should be the same as that of Christ Jesus:

Participants: Who, being in very nature God, did not consider equality with God something to be grasped,

Leader:	but made Himself nothing, taking the very nature of a servant, being made in human likeness.
Participants:	And being found in appearance as a man, He humbled Himself and became obedient to death—even death on a cross!
Leader:	Therefore God exalted Him to the highest place and gave Him the name that is above every name,
Participants:	that at the name of Jesus every knee should bow, in heaven and on earth and under the earth,
Leader:	and every tongue confess that Jesus Christ is Lord, to the glory of God the Father (Philippians 2:5–11).
All:	O Lord and Heavenly Father, You have given us the true Bread that comes down from heaven, Your Son Jesus Christ. Grant that our souls may be so fed by Him who gives life to the world that we may abide in Him and He in us and Your church be filled with the power of His unending life; through Jesus Christ our Lord. Amen.

Introduction

Modern songs played on the radio often declare the latest life-philosophy. One song declares, "You can do magic; you can do anything your heart desires." Some pop philosophers even suggest that we can become gods. Certainly God has provided each of us with gifts and abilities which should be developed to their fullest and to His glory. This is a far cry, however, from becoming gods.

It's one thing for a car to be fine-tuned so it can deliver the performance for which it was designed. It's another thing to suggest that the car can become the driver. What happens when the car breaks down? Or when its performance begins to lag? What happens when it simply needs gas or an oil change? It is helpless without the owner.

1. Briefly list some basic things for which we are completely dependent upon God.

2. Almost from the beginning Satan has tempted people with the notion that we can be like gods (Genesis 3:5). Ultimately, what happens to those who buy into this outwardly appealing philosophy (Proverbs 14:12)?

3. Sin is a condition that permeates our very nature. It is both inherited disobedience and actual disobedience. It is the root cause of all imperfect and fractured relationships. David's sin of adultery with Bathsheba deeply injured his relationship with others around him. How did it affect his relationship with God? See Psalm 51:3–6.

4. "Empowerment" is a popular buzz-word today. The effect of sin is the very opposite of empowerment. It leaves us powerless. Can you think of a particular instance when a certain sin consumed an individual? Read Psalm 9:15.

5. Sin leaves people paralyzed and powerless. It affects us spiritually, emotionally, mentally, and physically. The message of the Gospel, however, is liberating and life-giving. Contrast all we have said about sin and its effects with the words of Romans 5:6 and 8:3. What—or, rather, who—makes the difference? You or … ?

Inform

Read the following summaries of the Scripture lessons for the Sixth Sunday in Lent.

Isaiah 50:4–9—These are the words of the Servant, the Promised Messiah. He comes to sustain the weary. The Servant looks ahead to what He must bear for the weary. He will be mocked and condemned. Yet He does not draw back. In fact, His resolve is such that He sets His face like flint and assumes the role of servant who would atone for the sin of the world.

Philippians 2:5–11—St. Paul shows us Jesus as servant. He became one of us and was obedient to the task His Father had given Him. And such a task! It meant death on the cross. By that death on the cross, however, the dividing wall of sin is broken down. God's will is that, at the name of Jesus, all will proclaim Him Lord.

Matthew 27:11–54—The Gospel Lesson is an account of the trial of Jesus, the release of Barabbas, the crucifixion of Jesus, and His death. The Gospel of Matthew was written for a Jewish audience. This Gospel account, however, shows that Christ died for all: a centurion and others guarding Jesus confess that He truly was the Son of God.

1. The Servant speaks of "the word that sustains the weary." Who are the weary? What makes them weary? Read Psalm 63:1; 119:28; and Jeremiah 9:5.

2. What is the "word that sustains the weary?" Read Matthew 11:28.

3. Philippians 2:5–11 sets forth Jesus as the example of the perfect servant. It says that our attitude should be like His. Is that possible? How would you have felt if God had caused Paul to write no further than verse 5? What is there in verses 6–11 that is so vital to a proper understanding of verse 5?

4. What kind of obedience is required to deserve eternal life? See Matthew 19:17. Why could that be bad news for us? What alternative does God provide? See Philippians 2:8.

5. Compare the Gospel Lesson with the Old Testament Lesson. Look for the New Testament fulfillment of the Old Testament prophecy.

6. Sin separates us from God. In Matthew 27:46, we read that Jesus experienced that separation. Pilate and his wife declared Jesus innocent (Matthew 27:19; John 19:4). The Bible tells us that Jesus was without sin (Hebrews 4:15). Yet God forsakes His own Son because of sin. Whose sin? Read 1 John 2:1–2.

7. What is our connection with the events recorded in the Gospel Lesson? Read Romans 6:2–3.

Connect

1. Have you ever had to carry a large suitcase or other heavy burden for a great distance? What a relief it is to put it down. What an even greater relief for someone to offer to carry it for you. What a welcome servant that person would be! People often carry the oppressive burden of guilt because of sin. Take a moment and think of the things that you have done in your life that perhaps still bother you. They are like a heavy burden that wearies us.

What words from the Servant and about the Servant set us free from that burden?

2. Discuss last Sunday's worship service. Note the times when the Pastor spoke burden-lifting words.

3. In the Nicene Creed, we confess, "Who for us men and for our salvation." All the religions of the world talk about what man must do for God to earn salvation. Christianity teaches what God has done for us to earn our salvation. What verses from the lessons this week highlighted this scriptural truth for you?

4. Jesus clearly took our place at the cross. This isn't some sugar-coated religious myth with a moral teaching intended to improve our behavior. It is a real historical event. It shows the ugly, horrible consequence for sin and, at the same time, gives comfort and certainty about eternity because He did it "for you." Whom do you know that is carrying a heavy burden of sin and really needs to hear this message?

Vision

During This Week

1. Be sensitive and aware of people who are on a "guilt trip" and look for opportunities to share the good news of the Savior with them.

2. Is there a sin from your past that continues to bother you? It's time to let go! Read the Gospel accounts of the crucifixion of Jesus and remember that this was done for you to relieve you of your guilt. Perhaps you may wish to speak privately to the pastor and receive a personal word of absolution.

3. Many people not only live under the burden of guilt, they also live under the burden of self-righteousness. They try and make themselves acceptable to God through their own good deeds. Good deeds are turned into a "have to" instead of a "want to." The New Age movement tells us that we should strive with our own abilities to be gods. Christ sets us free to live to the glory of God. During the week, try an "attitude check." Ask yourself why you are doing certain things and seek to do things in response to the power of God's grace in Jesus Christ.

Closing Worship

Pray or sing together "When I Survey the Wondrous Cross" (*LW* 114).

> When I survey the wondrous cross
> On which the Prince of Glory died,
> My richest gain I count but loss
> And pour contempt on all my pride.
>
> Forbid it, Lord, that I should boast
> Save in the death of Christ, my God;
> All the vain things that charm me most,
> I sacrifice them to His blood.
>
> See, from His head, His hands, His feet
> Sorrow and love flow mingled down.
> Did e'er such love and sorrow meet
> Or thorns compose so rich a crown?
>
> Were the whole realm of nature mine,
> That were a tribute far too small;
> Love so amazing, so divine,
> Demands my soul, my life, my all!

Scripture Lessons for Maundy Thursday

Read in preparation for Maundy Thursday Exodus 12:1–14; 1 Corinthians 11:17–32; and John 13:1–17, 34.

Session 7

Maundy Thursday

Exodus 12:1–14; 1 Corinthians 11:17–32; John 13:1–17, 34

Focus

Theme: *Eat, Drink, Be Served ... And Serve*

Law/Gospel Focus

People by nature seek personal advantage. Our world seems to be in a mad rush to control others—even God—in order to gain that advantage. Jesus, however, comes to us as Servant and Redeemer. He gives Himself to us in the Lord's Supper. We receive through this Holy Meal the forgiveness, life, salvation, and the power and motivation to serve Him and others.

Objectives

By the working of the Holy Spirit through the Word of God, we will be led to
1. confess our own self-centeredness and our attempts to gain personal advantage over others;
2. rejoice in the service that Christ renders to us as He feeds us with His body and blood in the Lord's Supper;
3. serve others in selfless love as Christ has served us.

Opening Worship

Pray the following responsive prayer, the Gradual for Maundy Thursday, based on Hebrews 9:12, 15; and Psalm 111:9:

Leader: [Christ] entered the Most Holy Place once for all by His own blood,
Participants: having obtained eternal redemption.
Leader: He is the mediator of a new covenant,
Participants: that those who are called may receive the promised eternal inheritance.
Leader: He provided redemption for His people;
Participants: He ordained His covenant forever. Amen.

Introduction

Have you ever noticed how people try to control others to gain personal advantage?

Three young girls were walking home in the late afternoon of a warm summer day. One of them invited the other two to come over to her place after supper for movies and a "sleep over." One responded, "I'd love to, but I know my mother won't let me. She says I'm too young. Wait a minute. You know how I can make myself cry. When she says 'no' I'll turn on the tears—I mean *really* turn them on. She'll feel so bad that she will finally give in."

A young man suggests to his girlfriend that, since his parents are gone for the weekend, they could spend the night together at his house. She hesitates. And then he drops the manipulative bomb: "If you really love me, you will … "

An office manager says to the accountant, "I've put some personal things on my expense account this month. If you want to keep your job, play with the figures so no one will find out."

1. Have you ever been the object of manipulating people? Have you ever manipulated people to serve your own interests?

2. The greatest villains of history are those who tried to gain control over others, who sought to be served rather than to serve. Think of individuals in this century who fit this description. Did this approach benefit others? Ultimately did this approach benefit the villains? Read Luke 12:20–21.

3. It is said that the earliest English missionaries to Africa forwarded their belongings in a coffin. They knew they would never return. They would lose their lives in the service of the Gospel. According to worldly standards, they were losers. Check out God's standard, however, in Daniel 12:3.

4. What was the purpose of Jesus' ministry? See Mark 10:45.

Inform

Look at the brief summaries of the Scripture lessons for Maundy Thursday.

Exodus 12:1–14 tells us of the last of the plagues against Egypt. The Egyptians sought to control Israel and keep the people as slaves. God's purpose was that they should be His people and that the Savior would come from them. This last plague is the death of the firstborn in Egypt. The blood of a lamb was to mark the doorframes of the houses of the Israelites so that the angel of death would pass over them and not slay their firstborn.

In 1 Corinthians 11:17–32, the church in Corinth is chastised for its abuse of the Lord's Supper. Some were viewing this sacred meal as an opportunity to eat and get drunk. They would charge ahead of others so that there was nothing left for those who came later. Through St. Paul, the Lord's Apostle, we have set before us the teaching on the Lord's Supper. Here we see that He who is truly Lord comes to us in the bread and the wine and gives us His own body and blood. In this precious gift, we receive forgiveness of all our sins. This is His "new covenant" for us. The Lord's Supper was instituted by Christ for no other reason than that He loves us.

John 13:1–17 and verse 34 tell of foot washing. While none of the disciples would offer to serve by performing the customary foot washing, Jesus assumed the role of their servant and washed their feet. He sets for them the example of servant and in that role encourages them to serve and love others as He did, enabled by the cross.

1. In order to save the lives of the Israelites, lambs were slaughtered and their blood painted on the doorframes of the Israleite's homes. Of what does the lamb remind you?

2. "And when I see the blood, I will pass over you." Read Romans 5:8–10. In what way does God "pass over" us?

3. In the Lord's Supper, Jesus gives "My body, which is for you … this cup [as] the new covenant in My blood." For what purpose do we receive the body and blood of Jesus? See Matthew 26:26–27.

4. What do we proclaim whenever we eat the bread and drink the cup? See 1 Corinthians 11:26.

5. Why did none of the disciples want to wash the others' feet? See Luke 9:46; 22:24.

6. In John 13:16, Jesus says that no servant is greater than his master. What are the implications of this for the first disciples and for us?

7. In John 13:34, Jesus tells us that we are to love one another as He has loved us. Can we be servants like Jesus? How is this possible? Read again 1 Corinthians 11:26.

Connect

In Palestine there are two great seas. Both are fed by the River Jordan. Both are located within the same mountain range. Yet they differ greatly. The Sea of Galilee has fresh water teeming with fish and fowl. Trees and flowers grow along its banks. The Dead Sea's barren shores support no living creatures. Birds flying overhead have been killed by the fumes from the poisonous waters.

The one reason for the great differences is that the first "gets to give" and the second "gets to keep." The Sea of Galilee receives the fresh waters from the northern part of the River Jordan and passes them on to the southern part of the Jordan at the lower end. The Dead Sea also receives the fresh waters from the Jordan, but it has no outlet, and therefore its waters are stagnant and deadly.

1. What is the life-giving water that we get in order that we may give?

2. What outlets are there for us in our church and community for Christian service (foot washing)?

3. Why is the Lord's Supper so important in our life of Christian service?

4. What do the following passages teach us about Christian service?
   • James 1:27

   • Luke 12:35

   • 2 Corinthians 9:13

5. For the world, greatness is measured in fame, fortune, and power. The secret to greatness is really found in Matthew 23:11.

6. When you serve others, who are you ultimately serving? See Matthew 25:40.

Vision

During This Week
1. Ask the pastor if there are people he is aware of who have special needs and whom you can assist.
2. Attend the Maundy Thursday service and receive the Lord's Supper for the forgiveness of sins and for the strengthening of your faith that the Holy Spirit might enable you to serve God.
3. Look for opportunities to help those in need, and do it in such a way that people see Christ. See Matthew 5:15.

Closing Worship
Read Psalm 68:1–6. Then read or sing together "Sent Forth by God's Blessing" (*LW* 247).

> May God arise, may His enemies be scattered;
>   may His foes flee before Him.
> As smoke is blown away by the wind,
>   may You blow them away;
> As wax melts before the fire,
>   may the wicked perish before God.
> But may the righteous be glad
>   and rejoice before God;
>   may they be happy and joyful.

Sing to God, sing praise to His name,
  extol Him who rides on the clouds—
His name is the LORD—
  and rejoice before Him.
A Father to the fatherless, a Defender of widows,
  is God in His holy dwelling.
God sets the lonely in families,
  He leads forth the prisoners with singing;
  but the rebellious live in a sun-scorched land.

Sent forth by God's blessing,
Our true faith confessing,
The people of God from His dwelling take leave.
The supper is ended. Oh, now be extended
The fruits of this service in all who believe.
The seed of His teaching,
Receptive souls reaching,
Shall blossom in action for God and for all.
His grace did invite us,
His love shall unite us
To work for God's kingdom and answer His call.

With praise and thanksgiving
To God ever living,
The tasks of our ev'ryday life we will face.
Our faith ever sharing,
In love ever caring,
Embracing His children of each tribe and race.
With Your feast You feed us,
With Your light now lead us;
Unite us as one in this life that we share.
Then may all the living
With praise and thanksgiving
Give honor to Christ and His name that we bear.

Scripture Lessons for Good Friday

Read in preparation for Good Friday Isaiah 52:13–53:12; Hebrews 4:14–16; 5:7–9; and John 18:1–19:42.

Session 8

Good Friday

Isaiah 52:13–53:12; Hebrews 4:14–16; 5:7–9;
John 18:1–19:42

Focus

Theme: *Six-Point-O*

Law/Gospel Focus

God demands perfect obedience from us. As much as we
try, no matter what we do, we fail. On account of Jesus' perfect
obedience and His atoning sacrifice for our failures, God
declares us righteous.

Objectives

God is at work in His Word. As we study His Word the Holy
Spirit will lead us to

1. recognize our inability to live as God requires;
2. come to grips with the uselessness of trying to play "catch-up" with the Law in order to cover up past sin;
3. in faith, look to the life and death of Jesus as our only and certain hope;
4. live not as people who are dead in sin, but as people who have been made alive to God in Christ Jesus.

Opening Worship

Read responsively the following portions of the Old Testament and Epistle Lessons:

Leader: Surely He took up our infirmities and carried our sorrows, yet we considered Him stricken by God, smitten by Him, and afflicted.

Participants: We all, like sheep, have gone astray, each of us has turned to his own way; and the LORD has laid on Him the iniquity of us all.

Leader: For we do not have a high priest who is unable to sympathize with our weaknesses, but we have One who has been tempted in every way, just as we are—yet was without sin.

Participants: Yet it was the LORD's will to crush Him and cause Him to suffer, and though the Lord makes His life a guilt offering, He will see His offspring and prolong His days, and the will of the LORD will prosper in His hand.

Leader: Let us then approach the throne of grace with confidence, so that we may receive mercy and find grace to help us in our time of need.

Participants: After the suffering of His soul, He will see the light of life and be satisfied; by His knowledge My righteous servant will justify many, and He will bear their iniquities.

Introduction

The life of a figure skater is hard and arduous. For those who set their sights on world championships, it means long hours of strenuous practice every day. Every competition means the skater will be under the close scrutiny of audience and judges. Each stage of the competition—the compulsory figures, the short program, and the long program—presents formidable challenges. It is almost impossible to score a perfect 6.0 in any of these events. It is unheard of to attain a perfect score in all of them. The crowd continues to moan and sigh with each slip of the blade and unexpected trip on the ice. Only the best attain the coveted prize, and even at that, it is without a perfect program.

What would it be like to live constantly with expectations that can never be met? And we do live under the expectations of others. Parents, employers, teachers, spouse, family, even self, all have expectations of us. God also has expectations of us—high expectations. Jesus says "Be perfect, therefore, as your heavenly Father is perfect" (Matthew 5:48).

1. What is it like to know that your life is always less than a perfect "six-point-O?" What happens to people when they strive for but never achieve the perfection that is demanded of them?

2. Has anyone ever lived up to God's expectations? Read Romans 3:10.

3. Is it possible to "turn over a new leaf," to change one's life, and begin living according to God's Law in a way that will make us right with Him?

4. How serious is it when we fail to meet the demands of God's Law? Read Romans 6:23.

============================= **Inform** =============================

Read the following summaries of the Scripture lessons for Good Friday.

In Isaiah 52:13–53:12 God speaks through His prophet Isaiah and presents a picture of the Messiah. The purpose of His mission was not to win an earthly kingdom by virtue of "beauty or majesty." Rather, He came to pay for the sins and failures of all people. It was not a pretty picture. Yet it is "by His wounds [that] we are healed."

Hebrews 4:14–16 and 5:7–9 presents us with the sinless Son of God—the only one who could live a "six-point-O life." This perfect Savior is the source of eternal salvation. Through His obedience, we receive through faith, grace and forgiveness and are set free from the taskmaster of the Law. We are motivated and empowered by His grace to live to His glory.

John 18:1–19:42 is the account of the arrest, trial, crucifixion, death, and burial of Jesus. Although the death of Jesus was plotted to thwart His work, God's plan of salvation is carried out. With His dying breath, Jesus declares, "It is finished." The work of atonement is complete. All sin is paid for. Unaware of the scope of what has really transpired and what will soon take place, the world continues its business and Jesus is laid in the tomb of Joseph of Arimathea.

1. A great world leader has many distinctive attributes which make his leadership appealing to those who follow him. Would Jesus fit the bill? How does the Old Testament Lesson describe Him?

2. What are some pictures in the Old Testament Lesson that remind you of Jesus and the crucifixion?

3. What comfort is there in knowing that Jesus was tempted in every way, as we are, yet did not sin?

4. What is the difference between living under the Law and attempting to obey it, and living in obedience to Christ our Savior?

5. Make a list of all the people mentioned in the Gospel Lesson. Of all the people mentioned, which of them appeared to need Christ's forgiveness the most?

6. As you identified those who appeared to need forgiveness the most, what does that say about the measure of Christ's love for them? Does this surprise you?

Connect

Syndicated columnist Dave Barry writes,

> It was also a good year, spiritually, for us aging baby boomers; after too many years of being obsessively and selfishly absorbed with our own lives, we are finally starting to reach the point where we become obsessively and selfishly absorbed with our own deaths. This has led to a number of inspirational best-selling books about the afterlife— *Embraced by the Light, Saved by the Light, Garfield Sees the Light,* and *The Susan Powter Post-Mortem Workout.* (From *The Edmonton Journal,* 2 January 1995. [Reprinted by permission: Tribune Media Services])

How people try and search and struggle and strive! In fact, every religion in the world is an attempt to get closer to God. People change their lifestyle, pray more, seek spiritual experiences, and strive for a liberating spiritual enlightenment.

As we grow older, we become more aware of our mortality and our need to be "right with God." Looking at our sinfulness and then considering eternity can be a frightening experience. Fear, however, does not make us right with God.

Our problem is sin. It is the trash of our lives. There is no sense looking for treasure in it. The Christ of Calvary took our sin upon Himself and, at the cross, eliminated it. Jesus is the Way to the Father. The treasure, the new life, the "six-point-O" is found in Him.

1. The message of the cross is a liberating one. The Law demands a "six-point-O" life. The cross presents us with a "six-point-O" payment for our failures. Read Romans 8:1–4. What does this message do for the legalist and the libertarian?

2. Read John 3:16. God gave His Son so that all who believe in Him will have eternal life. We have received a "six-point-O" life from Jesus. The world may continue to send difficulties and hardships our way but nothing can rob us of what Christ has done for us. What even greater treasures can we look forward to from our Redeemer? Read Romans 8:18; Revelation 21:1–7; and 22:1–5.

Vision

During This Week

1. Attend Good Friday worship services with a friend. Recall your failures and ask for forgiveness in the shed blood of Jesus Christ.

2. Reevaluate your motivations. Have you been doing things out of fear of punishment or hope for reward? Start living a "six-point-O" life in the mercy and grace which come from Jesus.

Closing Worship

Pray or sing together "O Sacred Head, Now Wounded" (*LW* 113).

> O sacred head, now wounded,
>   With grief and shame weighed down,
> Now scornfully surrounded
>   With thorns, Your only crown.
> O sacred head, what glory
>   And bliss did once combine;
> Though now despised and gory,
>   I joy to call You mine!
>
> All this for my transgression,
>   My wayward soul to win;
> This torment of Your Passion,
>   To set me free from sin.
> I cast myself before You,
>   Your wrath my rightful lot;
> Have mercy, I implore You,
>   O Lord, condemn me not!

What language can I borrow
    To thank You, dearest friend,
For this Your dying sorrow,
    Your mercy without end?
Bind me to You forever,
    Give courage from above;
Let not my weakness sever
    Your bond of lasting love.

Lord, be my consolation,
    My constant source of cheer;
Remind me of Your Passion,
    My shield when death is near.
I look in faith, believing
    That You have died for me;
Your cross and crown receiving,
    I live eternally.

Scripture Lessons for Next Sunday

Read in preparation for Easter Sunday Acts 10:34–43; Colossians 3:1–4; and John 20:1–9 (10–18).

Session 9

The Resurrection of Our Lord

Acts 10:34–43; Colossians 3:1–4; John 20:1–9 (10–18)

Focus

Theme: *Razed to Be Raised!*

Law\Gospel Focus

Death without hope leads people to despair. Fear of death leads them to denial. But Jesus has conquered death by paying for sin and has declared us not guilty by reason of His grace and our God-given faith and given us life! Therefore His judgment of those who repent of their sins and believe in Him is "You have been raised!"

Objectives

That by the power of the Holy Spirit working in us through God's Word we might

1. realize that sin and death have the power to raze us spiritually;
2. recognize God's great love and grace toward us in Jesus Christ, who has raised us from sin and death by His own resurrection from the dead;
3. rejoice in our salvation and, motivated by God's love for us, seek every opportunity to share this good news with others.

Opening Worship

Sing or pray together "I Know that My Redeemer Lives," (*LW* 264).

> I know that my Redeemer lives!
> What comfort this sweet sentence gives!
> He lives, He lives, who once was dead;
> He lives, my Everliving Head!

He lives triumphant from the grave;
He lives eternally to save;
He lives exalted, throned above;
He lives to rule His Church in love.

He lives and grants me daily breath;
He lives, and I shall conquer death;
He lives my mansion to prepare;
He lives to bring me safely there.

He lives, all glory to His name!
He lives, My Savior, still the same;
What joy this blest assurance gives:
I know that my Redeemer lives!

Pray together,

Leader:	Christ is risen!
Response:	He is risen indeed!
Leader:	We thank You, Lord God, Heavenly Father, that Jesus died for all people and rose again from the dead so that all might live.
Response:	He is risen indeed!
Leader:	We praise You for our Lord Jesus and for His victory over sin, death, and the devil on this Easter Day!
Response:	He is risen indeed!
Leader:	We ask You to strengthen us today through the message of hope in Your Son's resurrection.
Response:	He is risen indeed!
Leader:	Christ is risen!
Response:	He is risen indeed!
All:	Christ is risen today, Alleluia! Amen!

Introduction

1. Define the word *raze.*

2. Define the word *raise.*

3. How was Jesus razed? What significance does this have for your life?

4. Jesus was raised three days after being razed. What significance does this have for your life?

5. How are we razed with Christ so that we are raised for eternity?

Inform

The mood of the followers of Jesus early Easter morning was one of sadness and despair as they struggled with the reality of His death. His body had been razed—destroyed—and His life ended, they thought. But, beginning with Mary at the tomb, all that changed. The mood became one of joyous celebration as she related that she had seen the Master and that He was indeed alive! As promised, God had raised Him from the dead, and they knew that victory over death, over sin, and over the devil had been won!

They knew that He had been razed by death, so to speak, so that one day they might be raised to eternal life.

Review the three Scripture lessons for Easter.

In the ancient world, when one nation conquered another and took its inhabitants into captivity it was also common for the victor to destroy the city in which its enemies lived. The conquering army would strip the city and its people of all their valuables and then systematically raze every building to the ground.

When, for example, the Romans finally conquered the people of Carthage after a long and costly war, so strong was their desire to remove the remembrance of these people from the face of the earth that they not only razed the city of Carthage but they sowed the land with salt so that no one might ever build a city again in that location.

With this picture in mind, consider the following questions.

1. How might the story of the razing of Carthage by the Romans serve as an allegory for the Roman treatment of Jesus? See Acts 10:39; John 19:17, 33–34; and Matthew 27:62–66.

2. Although Jesus' body was razed temporarily by death, who was it that was really razed by this event and Jesus' subsequent resurrection? See Genesis 3:15; 1 John 3:8; and Romans 16:20.

3. Describe the great assurance that we now have because Jesus razed Satan. Read 1 Corinthians 15:3–8 and 12–23.

   a. According to Paul, who was moved by the Holy Spirit to write this, how reliable is the teaching of the resurrection of Jesus Christ from the dead (vv. 3–8)?

   b. If Christ were not raised from the dead, what would that ultimately mean for Christians (vv. 13–19)?

c. What does it mean to you when Paul writes: "But Christ has indeed been raised from the dead, the firstfruits of those who have fallen asleep"?

4. In Colossians 3:1–4, what is it that St. Paul indicates has already happened to us? How has this happened? See Romans 6:3.

5. God reveals to us that the resurrection of Jesus also means a change of life for His people. How is that change of life described in our Epistle Lesson (Colossians 3:1–4)? See also Romans 6:2 and 11–18 and Galatians 5:13–14, 16–26.

6. Paraphrase the last verse of the Epistle Lesson. What do you think St. Paul is talking about when he writes: "When Christ, who is your life, appears, then you also will appear with Him in glory"? See also Matthew 24:30–31 and 1 Corinthians 15:51–57.

Connect

Because of our human nature and because God never intended human beings to die, there is a natural, built-in fear of death in each and every one of us. Read the following common fears that some people have shared and put a checkmark beside those that have affected you in the past.

1. I am afraid of *how* I will die.
2. I am afraid I will die alone.

3. I am afraid I will lose my faith.
4. I am afraid I will die in great pain and agony.
5. I am afraid that God will change His mind about me.
6. I am afraid that my doubting mind will overwhelm me.
7. I am afraid of dying on the operating table.
8. I am afraid of dying of AIDS.
9. I am afraid of what lies ahead after death.
10. I am afraid of the thought of my body lying in a grave.
11. Other: _____
12. Other: _____

These are but a few of the common fears that people express when contemplating their own death. If time allows, discuss those that people have checked. Then match the following Bible passages that offer hope and strength to a particular fear.

- Romans 8:38–39
- Matthew 28:20
- Joshua 1:5
- Jeremiah 1:8
- 1 Corinthians 15:42–49
- Ephesians 2:8–9
- Romans 5:3; 1 Peter 4:12–13, 19
- 1 Corinthians 2:5

God, through His revealed Word, removes from us the great fear of death. In the same way that Jesus returned to show Himself alive to His followers immediately after His resurrection from the dead, so today He comes to us through His Spirit-inspired Word and in the Sacrament of Holy Communion. In this way Jesus continues to give Himself to us today and fulfill His promise to be with us always. The fact is, we have a *living* Savior and that makes all the difference for us as we live our lives, slowly and surely moving toward physical death. Yes, physical death is a reality for us all, but thanks be to God who gives us the victory over death through our living Savior. Jesus alone removes the permanence of death from our life experience and impresses upon us forever, the reality of eternal life in heaven—by God's grace through faith in Him!

Take a few minutes, as time allows, to discuss in small groups or with another person the impact of the following Bible passages on you.

- 2 Timothy 1:10
- Colossians 1:21–23

- 1 Peter 3:18
- Romans 4:25–5:11

Vision

During This Week

1. When you get home, review this lesson and read any Bible passages that we could not cover in class. Then on a calendar, mark those opportunities that God gives you this week to share your joy and confidence in Christ's resurrection with friends or family members or even strangers. Remember, you need to be constantly aware of the opportunities that God will lay before you. Then be prepared next week to share any witnessing opportunities that may have come your way.

2. If you know of someone who has recently lost a loved one, write a letter of encouragement, perhaps utilizing some of the Bible passages that we shared here today. Be sure to point to Jesus, His cross, and His resurrection so that the grieving person may be uplifted and strengthened by the Word of God and your care.

Closing Worship

Pray together:

Dear Heavenly Father, we thank You for strengthening our faith and trust and hope in Jesus Christ for eternal life. When we approach our final days here on earth, please be with us and continue to strengthen our faith and trust in Your strong promises of forgiveness and eternal life in Jesus Christ, our Lord. Amen.

Scripture Lessons for Next Sunday

Read in preparation for the Second Sunday of Easter Acts 2:14a, 22–32; 1 Peter 1:3–9; and John 20:19–31.

Session 10

The Second Sunday of Easter

Acts 2:14a, 22–32; 1 Peter 1:3–9; John 20:19–31

Focus

Theme: *Restored Sight*

Law/Gospel Focus

By nature people are blind to the reality of God's revelation of Christ Jesus as risen Savior and Lord. But it is precisely the risen Lord who opens blind eyes and who, through the gift of faith, restores spiritual sight to those for whom He died.

Objectives

That by the power of the Holy Spirit working in us through God's Word we might

1. recognize our inability to see and understand the resurrection of Jesus Christ by ourselves;
2. receive by faith the truth of Scripture's revelation that Jesus Christ is our risen Savior;
3. proclaim the resurrection of Jesus Christ and His offer of salvation by grace through faith to others;
4. live a life that reflects our sure and certain hope of salvation in Christ alone.

Opening Worship

Pray together:

Leader: Lord, open our eyes to see Your resurrection as the fulfillment of all of God's promises of a Savior.

Participants: O Lord, open our eyes that we might see.

Leader: Gracious Heavenly Father, guide our study today in such a way that our faith and hope in Christ and His resurrection is strengthened.

Participants: O Lord, open our eyes that we might see.

Introduction

Sometimes human beings need help to see and sometimes no matter how hard they try to see, they just cannot. The obvious example is that of a person born blind. No matter how much that person may wish to see and may try to see, he or she simply cannot do so by sheer force of will. If, however, a qualified eye surgeon has determined that through an operation the person may receive his or her sight, and if that surgeon performs the needed surgery successfully, then the person's sight is restored. The point is, however, that an outside source is necessary for this to take place, and it will most likely cost the individual or a health-care system dearly.

It is often true also that there are things that a seeing person just cannot see by himself or herself. For instance, have you ever tried to see the picture contained in stereograms or 3-D art prints that have flooded bookstores across the country? Some people see the images immediately, others take a little longer, and some simply cannot see them at all. Whether it's birds on a canyon edge or dolphins in the sea, they cannot be seen at first glance but rather one must look "into" the picture. Then almost miraculously they appear so dramatically and realistically that a person feels that he or she can reach out and actually touch them.

In the same way, profound truths of God's Word often cannot be seen on the surface through ordinary eyes. The Holy Spirit working through God's Word and the Sacraments, reveals those truths to hearts and eyes that only He can open. Without the work of the Holy Spirit, you and I could never see or believe the reality of Jesus' resurrection, which is the key to understanding every other teaching in the Bible. But when the Holy Spirit does His work, the cross of Jesus, the empty tomb, and the resurrected Lord Jesus Christ Himself stand out in bold relief before the Christian's eyes—they become so real that one could almost touch them.

1. Have you seen the 3-D art mentioned above? If so, did you see

the 3-D image easily or only after some difficulty? Did anyone have to help you?

2. Have you ever known anyone who was blind from birth or because of cataracts, whose sight was restored by surgery? What was their reaction to receiving their sight?

The truth is that all of us from our birth are spiritually blind, and unless God Himself opens our spiritual eyes, they will remain forever closed to the truth of His love and forgiveness in Christ Jesus our Lord. Yet spiritual "eye surgery" is free for all people. The surgeon is the Holy Spirit, and His scalpel is the Gospel. That is how eyes blinded by sin are enabled to see once again!

═══ **Inform** ═══

Read the following summaries of the Scripture lessons for the Second Sunday of Easter.

Acts 2:14a, 22–32—The apostle Peter declares the persecution and death of Jesus took place according to God's plan. He delivers to his Jewish audience a scathing denunciation of their plot to join wicked people in their plan to kill God's Messiah, Jesus. Then Peter speaks a powerful proclamation of the reality of Jesus' resurrection and His fulfillment of all Old Testament prophecy concerning the Messiah who would come to redeem Israel.

1 Peter 1:3–9—Peter talks to Christians about their "new birth" through the resurrection of Jesus Christ from the dead. He emphasizes that our inheritance in heaven has been made certain by Jesus' resurrection. He also declares that even though we will experience hardships and trials in this life, our future in heaven has been secured through Jesus' resurrection.

John 20:19–31—John records the appearance of Jesus to His 11 disciples in the upper room shortly after His resurrection from the dead. Jesus offers them His "peace," gives them the Holy Spirit, and institutes the Office of Keys, that is, the power to forgive or retain sins. John also includes an account of Thomas' failure to believe that Jesus had risen from the dead and Jesus' subsequent appearance to Thomas and His offer to allow Thomas to touch His wounds. Most important are Jesus' words: "Because you have seen Me, you have believed; blessed are those who have not seen and yet have believed."

1. What does it mean that Jesus was "accredited by God to you by miracles, wonders, and signs"? See John 2:1–11; John 6:1–20; and John 11:38–44.

2. What does Acts 2:24 reveal about the manner by which Jesus was raised from the dead?

3. According to Acts 2:32, how sure was Peter that Jesus had actually risen from the dead?

4. According to 1 Peter 1:3, we are told that we have been given a "new birth into a living hope" because of the resurrection of Jesus.
   a. What is this "new birth" that Peter speaks of? See 2 Corinthians 5:17; Ephesians 4:24; and John 3:3–8.

   b. Have you received the "new birth" that Peter speaks of here? If so, when did it occur for you?

   c. If a person has not yet received the "new birth into a living hope," how could you be God's instrument to enable that to happen?

5. According to 1 Peter 1:5, what reassurance do we have that the "new birth" or faith in Jesus will endure the trials of our lifetime?

6. What is the purpose, according to 1 Peter 1:6, for the trials and temptations that come our way in life?

7. What verse(s) really connects 1 Peter 1 with our Gospel Lesson? Why?

8. Describe what can be learned from John's account of Jesus' appearance to His disciples, and especially to Thomas.

Connect

1. Has there ever been a time in your life when you felt a little like "doubting Thomas"? If so, describe what it felt like to doubt. What helped you deal with the doubts?

2. In today's scientific world—a world in which people demand empirical proof when someone makes a claim regarding something extraordinary—what does the Christian have to defend his or her belief in the resurrection of Jesus Christ? See Acts 1:8, Matthew 28:19, and 1 Corinthians 15:6.

3. Why do some people, despite the evidence, refuse to believe in Jesus Christ and His resurrection and even try to publicly discredit this truth? See Romans 1:18–24; 3:10–18, 23; and Ephesians 2:1–3.

4. Why is the resurrection of Jesus so important to us? What would life be like without it? How does it affect the daily life of every Christian? See 1 Corinthians 15:12–28.

Vision

During This Week

1. Each day read a portion of 1 Corinthians 15. Meditate on the promise of the Resurrection and all that it means to you.
2. Write a prayer that thanks God for raising Jesus from the dead, proclaiming victory for us over sin, death, and the devil, and for granting you faith in Him.

Closing Worship

Speak or sing together stanzas 1 and 5–8 of "O Sons and Daughters of the King" (*LW* 130).

Alleluia, alleluia, alleluia!
O sons and daughters of the King,
Whom heav'nly hosts in glory sing,
Today the grave has lost its sting!
Alleluia!

When Thomas first the tiding heard
That they had seen the risen Lord,
He doubted the disciples' word.
 Alleluia!

"My pierced side, O Thomas, see,
And look upon My hands, My feet;
Not faithless but believing be."
Alleluia!

No longer Thomas then denied;
He saw the feet, the hands, the side;
"You are my Lord and God!" he cried.
Alleluia!

How blest are they who have not seen
And yet whose faith has constant been,
For they eternal life shall win.
Alleluia!

Scripture Lessons for Next Sunday

Read in preparation for the Third Sunday of Easter Acts 2:14a, 36–47; 1 Peter 1:17–21; and Luke 24:13–35.

Session 11

The Third Sunday of Easter

Acts 2:14a, 36–47; 1 Peter 1:17–21; Luke 24:13–35

Focus

Theme: *Changed by Grace ... Excited by Faith*

Law/Gospel Focus

The Christian life is seen by some as boring and lacking in joy and excitement because it does not conform to the paradigms of the world. Christ injects great joy into the Christian's life as He reveals Himself to us and empowers us to respond in exciting Gospel outreach and service to God and people.

Objectives

That by the power of the Holy Spirit working in us through God's Word we might
1. understand the importance of keeping oneself separate from the world's philosophies and beliefs, which eventually lead to misery, pain, doubt and despair;
2. affirm the importance of being devoted to Christ, to regular worship, and to the truth revealed by God in His holy Word;
3. be propelled by the Holy Spirit beyond the joy of believing to the excitement of serving God and others with the Gospel in response to our God-implanted faith;
4. live joy-filled lives in love and service to God and understand this lifestyle as a response to the Gospel of Jesus Christ.

Opening Worship

Pray together:

Gracious Heavenly Father, we thank You for this day and the opportunities You will provide us to serve You and our neighbor. Please put the joy of knowing Jesus as our Savior and

Lord in our hearts, and the joy of sharing Your love in Christ on our tongues, so that we might be faithful witnesses of the truth to those around us.

Guide us as we study Your Word and grant us understanding that translates into a growing and confident faith, and a life that reflects that faith always. In Jesus' name. Amen.

Introduction

Ever since the Fall, people's lives have been characterized by hard work and often drudgery. And since that time people have sought ways in which to escape the work and drudgery of making a living, providing for their physical needs, and saving for a time when they will no longer be able to work.

When I was a young man, one of the temporary jobs that I had during the summer and other vacation times was piling wood in the sawmill at the Kroehler Furniture Company in Stratford, Ontario. My job was simple. I was to pick up two or three different lengths of wood that had been cut by the man on the swing-saw across from me, pile it on three-wheeled carts, and keep count. The work was terribly boring, and because of the noise of the saws and planers in the mill, you could not even chat with anyone as you worked. After a few days of piling wood in this way, I really did not want to do this any longer. But because I was attending college and soon the seminary, I had no choice—I needed the money, and so despite the boredom, I did the job.

There are many people today who are in the same position. They are working at jobs that give them little or no satisfaction, and so life often seems inconsequential and meaningless to them. They look for meaning and fulfillment and joy and excitement and hope for the future in other pursuits. And the world has lots to offer—the lights of Las Vegas, the films of Hollywood, the stages of Broadway, the glitter of Disney, and the lure of boats and snowmobiles. These all offer ways for human beings to escape the emptiness of life on this earth amidst billions of other people equally unhappy and searching for the one answer that will change everything.

But the answer to the tedium of life, the answer to living a full and productive and meaningful life can never be found in the philosophies, physical activities, or lifestyles of people, but only in the revelation of the Creator of it all.

When God reveals His plan for human beings, a plan that is all wrapped up in Christ, then we can really begin to enjoy life, for we can only experience joy-filled living in Jesus Christ. Jesus directs us to meaningful works of service in the world and excitement beyond description. As faith in Jesus' love and forgiveness grows, it produces caring acts of love and grace toward our fellow human beings that will often result in their coming to faith and abandoning the emptiness of the unbelieving world.

Inform

Read the summaries of the Scripture lessons for the Third Sunday of Easter.

Acts 2:14a, 36–47—At the end of Peter's account of the people's sin of crucifying the Lord of life, the Messiah, the Holy Spirit moves them to repent. They ask, "What shall we do now?" Peter tells them to be baptized for the forgiveness of all their sins and to separate themselves from the corrupt people who surround them. They engaged in regular fellowship, worship, and sharing of food and the Lord's Supper. Significantly, Luke ends with the words, "And the Lord added to their number daily those who were being saved."

1 Peter 1:17–21—Peter calls upon the believers to reject the thinking and the ways of the world and to, in effect, live as strangers in the world. He points out that they were redeemed by the blood of Jesus from the empty life characterized by conformity with the world. Because the believers have been brought to faith by the power of God who raised their Savior, Jesus, from the dead, their faith in God is solid and secure.

Luke 24:13–35—Two disciples of Jesus are on the road from Jerusalem to Emmaus after the crucifixion of Jesus. As they discuss the events of the passion and crucifixion, without knowledge of His resurrection, Jesus suddenly appears and begins to walk down the road with them. They do not recognize Him but allow Him to join in the conversation. Jesus explains to them His fulfillment of the prophecies of old regarding the death and resurrection of the Messiah, and then after eating a meal with them and opening their eyes to see who He really was, He suddenly disappears from view. These disciples returned immediately to Jerusalem, found the 11 disciples and those with them, and shared their experience with the risen Lord.

1. Immediately following the crucifixion of Jesus how do you think the disciples and other followers of Jesus felt? What uncertainties did they face?

2. If Jesus had not risen from the dead but stayed in the grave what would that have meant to the lives of those who believed? What would that have meant for us and our world today?

3. But in fact Jesus was alive. To whom did He reveal Himself alive? See Luke 24.

4. What was the response by the two disciples on the road to Emmaus when they realized they had been talking to Jesus? How did others respond as they encountered the risen Christ?

5. How do we respond as the living Lord and Savior Jesus Christ is revealed to us through Scripture?

6. As Peter shared the truth of a living Savior, a resurrected Savior, with the people in Jerusalem in Acts 2, how did they respond?

7. Remembering that Peter is writing to Jewish Christians, what do you think Peter means when he writes in his epistle that we have been "redeemed from the empty way of life handed down to you from your forefathers?"

Connect

All of these lessons focus on Jesus as the resurrected Lord. Through His resurrection people come to realize that He is alive! Knowing that one has a real and living God and Savior, not one made of innate wood and stone or of the imagination of a person's mind, makes a difference in how we look at life. How can a life that has as its foundation a sure and certain hope of eternal life in heaven, that has as its focus a real and living God and Savior, ever lack meaning and purpose, joy and direction? No, in Christ Jesus resurrected from the dead lies the purpose and direction for the meaningless existence of people who do not know why they are here and where they are going.

1. How does the reality of Jesus' resurrection affect your daily life?

2. The early Christians devoted themselves to the apostles' teaching, spent time in Christian fellowship, celebrated the Lord's Supper, worshiped together, and shared their resources so that they could proclaim the Gospel to others. Read Acts 11:19–26 and 13:1–3. Discuss together how your congregation still carries on with these activities of fellowship and mission. Are there areas where you need improvement?

3. By coming back again and again to Jesus and meeting Him in the Word and Sacraments, the early Christians were filled with excitement to share the Gospel and thus their lives were filled with meaning and great joy! Share ways in which your life is enriched by the Word and Sacraments and by your connection with fellow believers.

4. People all around us despair because their lives have not been touched by the love of God in Christ Jesus. Read Acts 1:7–8; 2:1–4; Romans 6:11–14; 8:1–4; and 10:14–15.
   a. Name some ways you and your fellow members have been reaching out to those without Christ in your community and in the world.

   b. List ways and means by which you could do more and encourage one another in faithful service to personally and collectively share the Gospel.

When heat is applied to water in a glass container we can watch as bubbles begin to form and excitedly rise to the top. They eventually become steam and enter the atmosphere. Likewise when Jesus our Savior is added to our lives, the excitement of faith produces bubbles of joy in His service—joy that rises to the surface and flows out of our lives into the atmosphere that surrounds us. Thus we affect others with the joy of salvation and become God's instruments to bring meaning and joy and hope to many.

Vision

During This Week

Pray daily for God to move you to hear faithfully the Word, remember your Baptism, receive the Lord's Supper regularly, and then to be ready to share your hope in Christ with others as He gives you the opportunity.

Closing Worship

End your time together by sharing one prayer request per person and ask for volunteers to pray for that need or request.

Scripture Lessons for Next Week

Read in preparation for the Fourth Sunday of Easter Acts 6:1–9; 7:2a, 51–60; 1 Peter 2:19–25; and John 10:1–10.

Session 12

The Fourth Sunday of Easter

Acts 6:1–9; 7:2a, 51–60; 1 Peter 2:19–25; John 10:1–10

Focus

Theme: *Dying to Live*

Law/Gospel Focus

The world offers life, but in reality it provides only death. Only Jesus Christ, by His death, provides life—abundant life here on earth and eternal life with Him in heaven.

Objectives

That by the power of the Holy Spirit working in us through God's Word we might

1. understand that all worldly philosophies and knowledge lead human beings to an eternal dead end;
2. be empowered by the Gospel to meet the challenges and seductions of the world's promises;
3. confess the promises of God in Christ Jesus wherever the circumstances allow—even if it means suffering for Jesus' sake.

Opening Worship

Read responsively the Introit for All Saints' Day and Commemoration of Martyrs.

Leader: These are they who have come out of the great tribulation;

Participants: they have washed their robes and made them white in the blood of the Lamb.

Leader: In You, O Lord, I have taken refuge;

Participants: let me never be put to shame, deliver me in Your righteousness.

Leader: Since You are my rock and my fortress,

Participants: for the sake of Your name lead and guide me.
Leader: Into Your hands I commit my spirit;
Participants: redeem me, O Lord, the God of Truth.
All: Glory be to the Father and to the Son and to the
            Holy Spirit; as it was in the beginning, is now, and
            will be forever. Amen.
Pray together the Collect for the Festival of St. Stephen:

Heavenly Father, grant us grace that in our sufferings
for the sake of Christ we may follow the example of Saint
Stephen, that we may look to Him who suffered and was
crucified on our behalf and pray for those who do us
wrong; through our Lord Jesus Christ, who lives and
reigns with You and the Holy Spirit, one God, now and
forever. Amen.

Introduction

Generally speaking, a basic operating principle of the world
around us is "Eat, drink, and be merry, for tomorrow you may die."
Such a shallow philosophy results in bumper stickers such as the one
that reads He Who Dies with the Most Toys Wins! More sobering is
the bumper sticker which reads He Who Dies ... DIES.

For the Christian, neither bumper sticker is fully true. The
inescapable truth for all of us, Christian and non-Christian alike is that
we will all die. This is true. It is borne out by experience and can be
proven scientifically. Everyone, someday, dies. There is no escape.
Death is inevitable.

This truth has been the source of fear for people of all ages and
times. Though we may seek ways to postpone it or even to deny it,
eventually all must face death. In its mad efforts to deny sin, death,
and the devil—and the reality of eternal death and hell—the world
promises life. It speaks through popular movies and songwriters,
through popular singers and actors. It tries mightily with all the power
of the media today to deny Christ, the reality of God, and the consequence of sin—death!

The world says: "If you really want to live a productive, happy, ful-
filling life just believe that you are a god and then live your life cen-
tering everything on yourself." This message of the New Age Move-

ment is really nothing more than the old heresies of Gnosticism and spiritism wedded and covered in new clothing. Whatever gives people pleasure, whatever makes them feel good—even at the expense of others—is the world's recipe for a great life.

The Word of God suggests that the opposite is true. Godly people have sought to counteract the world's views since the very beginning. History and experience alone tell us that life lived for oneself, life based on the false notion that we are "gods," life on one's own without God or Jesus Christ, leads not to life, but most certainly to death.

1. What are the differences and/or similarities between the phrases "living to die" and "dying to live?"

Christians are well aware that death looms in their future and could occur at any moment. But death is not the end for the Christian. Death is merely the last event we experience at the end of this earthly life as we prepare to enter the heavenly mansions prepared for those who believe in Jesus Christ alone for forgiveness and eternal life.

2. How do people today demonstrate they are dying to live? Living to die?

3. Use some or all of the following words to describe the life of Jesus: *living, live, dying, die.*

4. Use some or all of the following words to describe the life of a Christian: *living, live, dying, die.*

5. What other words or phrases might you use to describe the life of a Christian?

Today, we will discover how through faith in Christ Jesus the life of a Christian could be described as one who is dying to live.

Inform

The following are the summaries of the Scripture lessons appointed for the Fourth Sunday of Easter.

Acts 6:1–9; 7:2a, 51–60—Because the Greek Christians were concerned about the lack of care being provided for their widows and believed that they should have the same care as the Jewish Christian widows, the disciples decided to appoint men full of the spirit and wisdom to oversee the distribution of food to all the needy widows. Among them were Stephen, Philip, Procorus, Nicanor, Timon, Parmenas, and Nicolas, a convert from Antioch.

As the Word of God spread, the number of believers increased dramatically in Jerusalem. A large number of priests were also converting from Judaism to Christianity.

Stephen not only served by assisting with the distribution of food but he also performed miracles and proclaimed the Word of God. Great opposition arose from a group called "the Synagogue of the Freedmen" who were Jews of Cyrene and Alexandria, Cilicia and Asia. Stephen responded to them by pointing out that Jesus was the Messiah. He then stirred the pot of their anger as he accused his hearers of killing the Messiah by crucifying Him on Calvary.

As a result the angry Jews stoned Stephen to death. As he was dying God opened the heavens for him and he saw Jesus in all His kingly splendor, ruling over the universe. As he gave his spirit up into the hands of Jesus in death he said, "Lord, do not hold this sin against them."

1 Peter 2:19–25—Peter points out that there is no honor in suffering for the wrongs that one has done. However if one suffers for the sake of Christ, for doing and saying what is right, there is great honor and even commendation from God. Peter suggests that we

should not be surprised at having to suffer for the sake of Jesus, because in so doing we are merely walking in the steps of Him who first suffered for us.

Peter reminds us that when Jesus suffered for us He did not complain, and when insulted He did not respond in kind. In so doing He sets the example or pattern for us to follow when we suffer for the sake of the Gospel. He closes by reminding us that it is only by Jesus' wounds that we are healed and like sheep who have gone astray we have now been led back to "the Shepherd and Overseer of our souls."

John 10:1–10—Jesus here teaches us that He Himself is the only gate into the sheepfold of God. All others that came before Him and who come after Him claiming to be the Savior are robbers who come only to steal and kill and destroy the sheep. He ends by telling us that He has come so that we might have life to the full.

1. As you consider John 10:1ff., give examples of the kind of "thieves" or "robbers" that Jesus speaks about. Who were the "thieves" in the Acts lesson? What thieves lurk to rob us of our faith today?

2. What makes Jesus the "gate"? To what is Jesus the gate?

3. Compare what Stephen says in Acts 7:51–53 with Exodus 32:9, 33:3–5, and Jeremiah 10:25. Explain what God means when He calls the Israelites "uncircumcised in heart." See also Nehemiah 9:16.

4. Why did Stephen's comments enrage the Jews to whom he was talking?

5. Stephen sacrificed his life as God's prophet. This was nothing new. See Nehemiah 9:26 and Luke 11:47–48. According to the Epistle Lesson (1 Peter 2:19–25) was Stephen's death "commendable?" Why or why not?

6. Jesus reveals that He is the gate into the kingdom of God and that anybody who tries to enter by another means is nothing more than a "thief" or "robber." What does Jesus say will happen to those who enter through "the gate?"

7. What do you think Jesus meant when He said that He had come so that we might have "abundant" life?

Connect

1. List some ways people today suffer for the sake of Christ and the Gospel.

2. What are some of the things that the world offers us which would *keep* us from suffering for the sake of the Gospel and make life easy?

3. What are some of the messages that Christians proclaim to the world today that will not be popular?

4. The world holds out before our eyes a picture of what life should be like. Describe that picture as you see it. Where does such living eventually lead?

5. Jesus offers a very different picture of life. Describe the picture of "abundant" life as God reveals it to us in His Word.

Vision

During This Week

1. Take note of the offers of the "good life" being made in the media. Write what advertisers, talk-show guests, and television shows promote in order for your life to be full and complete.
2. Share your findings with your family. Discuss them during family devotions in the light of the three Bible readings for today.
3. Put your saying that describes your life in Christ on Post-It notes. Place them in conspicuous spots where you can review them often.

Closing Worship

Pray or sing together stanzas 1, 2, 6, 7, and 8 of "For All the Saints" (*LW* 191).

> For all the saints who from their labors rest,
> All who by faith before the world confessed,
> Your name, O Jesus, be forever blest.
> Alleluia! Alleluia!

You were their rock, their fortress, and their might;
You, Lord, their captain in the well-fought fight;
You, in the darkness drear, their one true light.
Alleluia! Alleluia!

The golden evening brightens in the west;
Soon, soon to faithful warriors comes their rest;
Sweet is the calm of paradise the blest.
Alleluia! Alleluia!

But then there breaks a yet more glorious day:
The saints triumphant rise in bright array;
The King of glory passes on His way.
Alleluia! Alleluia!

From earth's wide bounds, from ocean's farthest coast,
Through gates of pearl streams in the countless host,
Singing to Father, Son, and Holy Ghost:
Alleluia! Alleluia!

Scripture Lessons for Next Week

Read in preparation for the Fifth Sunday of Easter Acts 17:1–15;
1 Peter 2:4–10; and John 14:1–12.

Session 13

The Fifth Sunday of Easter

Acts 17:1–15; 1 Peter 2:4–10; John 14:1–12

Focus

Theme: *Christ the Cornerstone*

Law/Gospel Focus

By nature and apart from God we build our lives on foundations that have no cornerstone to give them strength and durability. But God provides the needed cornerstone for our lives in the person and work of Jesus Christ.

Objectives

That by the power of the Holy Spirit working in us through God's Word we might

1. survey the foundation and cornerstone upon which we have been building our lives;
2. recognize that the only foundation that will allow Christ to be the cornerstone is the foundation of the prophets and apostles as revealed by God in His Word;
3. confess Jesus Christ alone to be the Cornerstone of our lives and build everything upon Him.

Opening Worship

Sing or pray together, "The Church's One Foundation" (*LW* 289).

> The Church's one foundation
> Is Jesus Christ, her Lord;
> She is His new creation
> By water and the Word.
> From heav'n He came and sought her
> To be His holy bride;
> With His own blood He bought her,
> And for her life He died.

Elect from every nation,
    Yet one o'er all the earth;
Her charter of salvation:
    One Lord, one faith, one birth.
One holy name she blesses,
    Partakes one holy food,
And to one hope she presses
    With ev'ry grace endued.

Through toil and tribulation
    And tumult of her war
She waits the consummation
    Of peace forevermore
Till with the vision glorious
    Her longing eyes are blest,
And the great Church victorious,
    Shall be the Church at rest.

Yet she on earth has union
    With God, the Three in One,
And mystic sweet communion
    With those whose rest is won.
O blessed heav'nly chorus!
    Lord, save us by Your grace
That we, like saints before us,
    May see You face to face.

Pray together: O Lord, Jesus Christ, our only sure cornerstone in life, grant the power of Your Holy Spirit upon us as we study and learn together today. Calm our hearts for concentrated and consecrated learning as we step out of our busy schedules and take the time to gather around Your holy Word. Teach us so that we might learn more of Your love and be prepared to share that love with one another and with others not yet of the household of faith. We ask these things in Your most precious name. Amen.

Introduction

Recently a pastor moved from Langely, British Columbia, to Stony Plain, Alberta, Canada. He received and accepted a call to a dual parish in the area of Stony Plain and began searching for a home. A beautiful, relatively new home in a new subdivision was on the market, and he and his wife decided to buy it. There was great joy when they moved into their beautiful new home, and for many weeks they enjoyed living in it.

However, when a particularly heavy rain fell one day, the family noticed water seeping through the foundation. Soon they discovered that there was a large crack in the foundation of their new home. Immediately they knew they could waste no time in having it repaired, because the fate of the entire house rested upon the strength of that foundation to withstand the rains and minus 40-degree weather in winter.

That pastor had trusted those selling the home and was ripped off because the former owners failed to reveal the structural defect.

In the world today there are many who are intent upon ripping us off spiritually. If we fall prey to them, we lose not just a house, but we lose the eternal life which God has prepared for those who believe His message of salvation in Jesus Christ alone.

1. What today could cause us to lose or to rob us of our faith?

In our spiritual lives we can build on a worldly foundation of the thoughts and musings of humans or we can build upon the foundation of the teachings of the prophets and apostles of God. That foundation does have a cornerstone and that is the chief cornerstone, Jesus Christ. Without Him nothing can stand. Nothing can destroy that which has been built on Him.

2. What supports a faith that is firmly grounded in Christ Jesus?

Inform

The following are the summaries of the Scripture lessons appointed for the Fifth Sunday of Easter.

Acts 17:1–15—At Thessalonica the apostle Paul began to proclaim the Gospel of Jesus Christ in the synagogue, and many Greeks and Jews came to faith. But the Jews who refused to believe that Jesus was the Messiah stirred the people of Thessalonica up against Paul and Silas. When they could not find Paul and Silas they dragged Jason, their host and some others before the city officials and made them post bond. The Jews accused Paul and Silas of defying the decrees of Caesar.

Paul and Silas traveled to Berea sharing the Gospel there, and once again many conversions occurred. The Bereans also checked out what Paul was preaching with the Scriptures and found it to be in complete agreement. Paul and Silas, having been harassed by the Jews from Thessalonica once again, departed and went to Athens.

1 Peter 2:4–10—Peter calls Jesus the "living stone" and declares that as we come to Him in faith, we, too, become like living stones being built up into a spiritual priesthood. By quoting the Old Testament Peter shows how Jesus is the fulfillment of Old Testament promises and prophecy regarding God's promise to lay a cornerstone in Zion. He says that the builders rejected the cornerstone, and it has become a stumbling-block to them. He then calls those who do believe "a chosen people, a royal priesthood, a holy nation, a people belonging to God." Through faith we can truly praise our God who has taken us out of the darkness of unbelief and into the light of faith.

John 14:1–12—Jesus promises to prepare a place for us and all believers in the mansions of heaven. He clearly says that He alone is the Way to those mansions. He is the way, the truth, and the life. He is also the physical manifestation of God the Father among the disciples. Jesus explains that they have seen the Father when they look at Him because He and the Father are one. Jesus ends this section of Scripture with the promise that His hearers would do greater things than He did after He returns to the Father.

1. What do you think Peter means when he talks about a "living" stone? To what or to whom does this refer?

2. Peter calls believers living stones also. How does one become a "living" stone?

3. The priesthood described here by Peter is the fulfillment of God's Old Testament prophecy. Read Exodus 19:6 and Isaiah 61:6. How was the prophecy fulfilled?

4. As living stones we are being built into a holy priesthood that offers "spiritual sacrifices acceptable to God." What are these "spiritual sacrifices" to which Peter refers? See Hebrews 13:15–16; and Hosea 6:6.

5. For whom has the "Cornerstone" become a stone that causes people to stumble?

6. According to 1 Peter 2:9, what is our status as Christians? What is our God-given task?

7. In the Acts 17 passage who are
a. those for whom Jesus the Messiah became a stumbling block?

b. the royal priesthood … the holy nation … the people of God?

8. Describe how Jesus reveals Himself as the "chief cornerstone" in John 14. What makes Jesus the one upon whom everything else depends?

Connect

1. Does it still hold true that Jesus Christ is a "stone of stumbling" for people today? Why or why not?

2. What does it mean to you that Jesus is *your* chief cornerstone? How does Jesus make the difference in your faith and life?

3. Since God has made us who believe in Jesus as Savior His "royal priests," a "holy nation," and "a people belonging to God," how will we live and what will we do with our lives? See 1 Peter 2:9b; Ephesians 2:10; Ephesians 4:24; Romans 6; and Acts 1:8.

4. As the royal priests of God through faith in Jesus, should we expect that our lives will be easy? What does Acts 17:1–15 tell us to expect if we faithfully proclaim the risen Christ to the world?

5. In the following Bible passages, God makes promises regarding what we can expect from Him if we are about His business. Fill in the blank at the right with His promise.

Bible Passage   *Promise*
Matthew 28:20
Luke 12:11–12
Romans 8:38–39
Luke 21:12–13

Vision

During This Week

1. Give yourself a spiritual checkup by answering these questions:
   a. What things in your life are so important to you that if you lost them your life would fall apart?
   b. What is truly the "cornerstone" of your life?
   c. How does the time you spend on activities in your life reflect your spiritual priorities?
   d. How do you serve God and others in response to God's love for you in Christ? Include family, friends, and others currently outside your circle of acquaintances.
   e. How does your life reflect your belief that God will be with you and bless you in all that you do as His servant?
2. After you honestly answer the questions get together with another member of the class or a close friend and ask them to discuss these questions with you. How accurately do you see yourself and your Christian life? How do others see you? How can you improve?

Closing Worship

Sing or pray together, "Take My Life, O Lord, Renew" (*LW* 404).

Take my life, O Lord, renew,
Consecrate my heart to You;
Take my moments and my days;
Let them sing Your ceaseless praise.

Take my hands and let them do
Works that show my love for You;
Take my feet and lead their way,
Never let them go astray.

Take my voice and let me sing
Praises to my Savior King;
Take my lips and keep them true,
Filled with messages from You.

Take my silver and my gold,
All is Yours a thousandfold;
Take my intellect, and use
Ev'ry pow'r as You shall choose.

Make my will Your holy shrine,
It shall be no longer mine.
Take my heart, it is Your own;
It shall be Your royal throne.

Take my love; my Lord, I pour
At Your feet its treasure store;
Take my self, Lord, let me be
Yours alone eternally.

Scripture Lessons for Next Sunday

Read in preparation for the Sixth Sunday of Easter Acts 17:22–31;
1 Peter 3:15–22; and John 14:15–21.

Session 14

The Sixth Sunday of Easter

Acts 17:22–31; 1 Peter 3:15–22; John 14:15–21

Focus

Theme: *Living on Purpose*

Law/Gospel Focus

Without Christ in our lives we drift like a ship without a rudder, for we have no purpose. Christ forgives us for our disobedience and disregard for His direction in our lives. Through faith, He becomes our rudder in life, provides us with a purpose for living, and gives us our direction.

Objectives

That by the power of the Holy Spirit working in us through God's Word we might

1. see clearly the reason why the world around us seems to change constantly and fails to provide the positive, in-depth direction for life that human beings need;
2. compare and contrast the meaninglessness that results from faith in the world's teachings and the meaningful life that results from faith in Christ;
3. share with the unbelieving world around us the hope in Christ that gives our lives meaning and purpose.

Opening Worship

Read Hebrews 6:13–20 aloud. Then sing or speak together "My Hope Is Built on Nothing Less" (*LW* 368).

> My hope is built on nothing less
> Than Jesus' blood and righteousness;
> No merit of my own I claim
> But wholly lean on Jesus' name.

Refrain
On Christ, the solid rock, I stand;
All other ground is sinking sand.

When darkness veils His lovely face,
I rest on His unchanging grace;
In ev'ry high and stormy gale
My anchor holds within the veil. *Refrain*

His oath, His covenant, His blood
Sustain me in the raging flood;
When all supports are washed away,
He then is all my hope and stay. *Refrain*

When He shall come with trumpet sound,
Oh, may I then in Him be found,
Clothed in His righteousness alone,
Redeemed to stand before the throne! *Refrain*

Introduction

The world is full of people who have absolutely no idea why they are here. They have no sense of purpose. They believe that life is something that you just pass through, during which you try to experience as many good times as possible, and then die. These people inhabit every walk of life, every profession, and every economic level in society.

1. What do all of these people have in common?

2. How are all these people like ships without rudders?

3. Is this a totally foreign experience to the person who has been a lifelong Christian, who believes in and follows Jesus? How might the Christian be caught in a rudderless trap?

4. What assurance do Christians have even when at times their lives seem to lack purpose? See 1 John 1:9.

Through Christ we "live on purpose." Our lives are not an aimless drift. The mysteries of the world do not occupy our minds because the greatest mystery, that of the purpose of human beings and the provision God has made for eternal life in Christ, has been revealed by God Himself.

Inform

The following are the summaries of the Scripture lessons appointed for the Sixth Sunday of Easter.

Acts 17:22–31—St. Paul is in Athens, the seat of ancient philosophers. At the Areopagus, Paul speaks to the men who have gathered to discuss the great questions of the day. He compliments them on their religiosity and notes the statue to an "unknown god" at the Areopagus. Paul uses this statue to reveal the true God to the men of Athens. He explains that this God cannot be seen or represented by statues and that He is the Creator of all things. He concludes by telling the men that this God calls them to repent because there will come a time when He will come and judge the earth.

1 Peter 3:15–22—Peter encourages us to set apart Christ in our hearts and to be prepared to give an answer to any who asks about the hope that we have as Christians. He tells us to share our hope with gentleness and respect. He reminds us that Christ, the Righteous One, was put to death in our place and made alive by the Spirit. Then

he compares the waters of the Flood to the waters of Baptism, reminding us that Baptism has the power to save us as it connects us with the resurrection of Jesus.

John 14:15–21—Jesus tells us that if we love Him we will keep His commands. He tells us that because He lives we too will live. The world cannot accept the Holy Spirit because it does not know of Him, but we know Him because He lives in us.

1. The Areopagus was a public gathering place where the great philosophies of the day were discussed in the city of Athens. Surrounding the Areopagus were statues of every known god in the Greek and Roman world. To be sure that no god was overlooked there was even a statue dedicated to the "unknown god"—just to be safe. It was into this place of thinkers and debaters that Paul came to share the Gospel. How does St. Paul use what the people in the Areopagus are familiar with in order to get their attention? How might we use Paul's approach to share the good news of Jesus Christ with unbelievers?

2. What is Paul's purpose in coming to this place?

3. In Acts 17:29 what new insight does Paul share with his audience?

4. How were the men in the Areopagus "adrift" in the world and lacking direction for their lives?

5. Peter reminds us in 1 Peter 3:15–22 that we are to be ready to give the reason for our hope. How does he urge us to share the reason for our hope? Read Romans 10:14–15.

6. To what does Peter compare the waters of the Flood? Why is this comparison important to us?

7. Much of our hope comes from our Baptism. According to Peter, what is the reason for that hope?

8. Because we love Jesus, what does He say in our Gospel Lesson that we will do? What are some things that we do or refuse to do in our everyday lives as we are moved to demonstrate our love to Jesus because of what He has done for us?

Connect

1. Make a list of some of the ways in which we are tempted by the world to build our lives on foundations and cornerstones other than Jesus Christ.

2. Paul's reminder that God is a God of judgment would have struck a certain amount of fear into the hearts of the men of the Areopagus. Does it do the same to us? Why or why not?

3. Can you think of an instance when you had the opportunity to tell someone about Jesus, to express your faith in Him, but did not? Is this a common occurrence in our lives? What is God's response when we do not witness when given the opportunity? See Psalm 103:12; Romans 4:7; and Ephesians 2:4–5.

4. As Noah passed through the waters of the Flood and was saved by the grace of God, so too we pass through the waters of Baptism and are saved by the grace of God. What are we connected to by Baptism that gives us absolute assurance that we are saved for all eternity? See 1 Peter 3:21.

5. Discuss together how we can daily live "on purpose" rather than just let life happen.

Vision

During This Week

1. When temptations or trials come this week remind yourself of 1 Peter 3:21–22.
2. Take some notes on the pastor's sermon, especially if he chooses

one of the appointed readings for his text. During the week reread your notes on his sermon and the Scripture passages we have studied.

3. Talk with your family or friends this week in devotion time about your direction in life and theirs. Direct one another to Jesus and allow Him to strengthen you and uplift you and help you to live your life on purpose.

Closing Worship

Pray the following prayer:

Dear Heavenly Father, thank You for enlightening our minds with Your Word today and for strengthening our faith in Jesus. Help us daily to put our full trust in You for forgiveness, salvation, and direction for our daily life.

Thank You, Lord for always being there when we need You and for always loving us and forgiving us for Jesus' sake when we sin. Amen.

Scripture Lessons for Next Sunday

Read in preparation for Ascension of Our Lord Acts 1:1–11; Ephesians 1:16–23; and Luke 24:44–53.

Session 15

The Ascension of Our Lord

Acts 1:1–11; Ephesians 1:16–23; Luke 24:44–53

Focus

Theme: *Whom You Know! What You Know!*

Law/Gospel Focus

People often live by the motto "It's not what you know, but whom you know that enables you to get ahead." This notion is sinful when it blindly ignores or forgets Him who will ultimately enable you to get that which will lead to eternity. By God's grace through faith in the one whom God has made known to us—Jesus Christ—we receive forgiveness of sins and eternal life with Him in heaven. The Holy Spirit enables us to confess, "It's not only what you know, but whom you know—the work and person of Jesus—that will enable you to know who you are and what you are to be about."

Objectives

That by the power of the Holy Spirit working in us through God's Word we might

1. identify the forces and factors that cause people to seek getting ahead as the highest goal of their lives;
2. recognize that improving one's lot in life is not wrong unless it overshadows or ignores the one who is able to provide eternal blessings;
3. reaffirm that Christ provides the best that life can offer— eternal life in heaven.

Opening Worship

Speak responsively the Introit for the day.
Leader: God has ascended amid shouts of joy,
Participants: the Lord amid the sounding of trumpets.

Leader: The Lord says to my Lord:
Participants: "Sit at My right hand, until I make Your enemies a footstool for Your feet."
Leader: The Lord has sworn and will not change His mind:
Participants: "You are a priest forever, in the order of Melchizedek."
Leader: The Lord is at your right hand;
Participants: He will crush kings on the day of His wrath.
All: Glory be to the Father and to the Son and to the Holy Spirit; as it was in the beginning, is now, and will be forever. Amen.

Pray The Collect for the day:

Grant, we pray, almighty God, that even as we believe Your only-begotten Son, our Lord Jesus Christ, to have ascended into heaven, so we may also in heart and mind ascend and continually dwell there with Him who lives and reigns with You and the Holy Spirit, one God, now and forever. Amen.

Introduction

"It's not *what* you know but *whom* you know that is important."

A Lutheran high school band and choir from Saginaw, Michigan, were trying to get across the border into Canada. The border guards demanded thousands of dollars from the director "to insure that they would not sell the instruments in Canada." No matter how hard the director pleaded, the border officials would not listen. He appealed to their common sense, indicating that if band members sold their instruments, they would be unable to play in the concert.

A chaperon traveling with the band had assisted a local Presbyterian pastor in his campaign to become a member of Parliament. The pastor-turned-politician was now Secretary of State and his assistance was requested by the chaperon. Within 10 minutes the band and the choir were given permission to enter Canada with no deposit on their instruments. Sometimes *who* you know makes a big difference!

1. What situations have caused you or someone you know to exclaim, "It's not what you know but whom you know that is important?"

2. How does the phrase, "It's not *what* you know but *whom* you know," relate to your faith life?

3. Would the phrase, "It's not only *what* you know but *whom* you know," more accurately reflect your faith life? Why or why not?

Inform

Read the following summaries of the Scripture lessons appointed for Ascension Sunday.

Acts 1:1–11—Luke recounts the resurrection appearances of Jesus and His promise to send the Holy Spirit upon them. Jesus also states clearly that the disciples will be His witnesses after they receive the gift of the Spirit. They will witness to Him in Jerusalem, Judea, Samaria, and to the ends of the earth. After speaking to them, He suddenly is taken up before their eyes into the heavens until a cloud hides Him from their sight. An angel then appears and reassures them that Jesus will one day return in the same way they saw Him leave.

Ephesians 1:16–23—St. Paul prays for the spiritual strengthening of the people at Ephesus. He assures the people that God is using the same power that He used to raise Jesus from the dead in order to give them spiritual strength. He reveals here that Jesus is indeed in the heavenly places with His Father and that He is now ruling over all creation because God has placed all things under His feet.

Luke 24:44–53—In this Gospel Lesson Jesus opens the eyes of the disciples to understand the prophecies regarding how the Messiah would suffer and die and rise again on the third day. He explains that they are now the witnesses of these things which have occurred before their own eyes. He promises to send the Holy Spirit who will cloth them with power. Then, as in the Acts account Jesus is taken up into heaven before their eyes. They responded by worshiping Jesus and then returned to Jerusalem and praised God in the temple.

1. How long, according to the Acts lesson, did Jesus appear to people and continue to speak to them about the kingdom of God? What is significant about this length of time? See Genesis 7:4, 12; Exodus 16:35; Exodus 24:18; and Matthew 4:2.

2. Describe what the disciples experienced on the mount at the ascension of our Lord into heaven. Use both the Acts reading and the Gospel Lesson as your guide.

3. Why do you think that God provided angels immediately after Jesus' ascension to speak to the disciples? See also Luke 1:28–38; Luke 2:9–14; Matthew 1:20–23; Matthew 2:13; and Matthew 4:11.

4. What does it mean when Luke writes that Jesus "opened their minds" (v. 45)? Why could they not understand these things before?

5. What do you think is significant about Paul's statement to the Ephesians that God "seated Him at His right hand in the heavenly realms?"

6. After the appearance of the angels and the disappearance of Jesus, what was the reaction of the disciples?

Connect

1. Why is it imperative that we know both *the who* and *the what* about Jesus?

2. We have been "clothed with power from on high" (Luke 24:49). For many of us that occurred as the Holy Spirit brought us to faith at our Baptism. Others were "clothed with power" as the Holy Spirit brought them to faith as they heard God's Word proclaimed. Because we have received this power from on high, what do we learn from these three lessons about who we are and what we are to be about?

   • Acts 1:8

   • Ephesians 1:17

   • Ephesians 1:18–19

   • Luke 24:48

   • Luke 24:49

   • Luke 24:52–53

3. Jesus ascended into heaven and took His place at the right hand of the Father. How does this fact affect *who* you are and *what* you know and do?

4. What assurance does God provide when we are tempted to forget *who* we know and *what* we know about Him or when we forget *who* we are through faith and *what* we are to be about?

Vision

During This Week

1. Read Revelation 21 and 22. Meditate on the message of salvation contained therein and picture in your mind's eye the beauty of what God has prepared for you in heaven through faith in Christ Jesus.
2. Share your insights regarding *who* you are and *what* you are empowered to do because of *who* you know—Jesus Christ—and *what* you know about Him with a person who needs strengthening of their faith. Pray for that person.

Closing Worship

Join together in singing "I'm but a Stranger Here" (*TLH* 660).

> I'm but a stranger here,
> Heav'n is my home;
> Earth is a desert drear,
> Heav'n is my home.
> Danger and sorrow stand
> Round me on ev'ry hand;
> Heav'n is my fatherland,
> Heav'n is my home.

What though the tempest rage,
Heav'n is my home;
Short is my pilgrimage,
Heav'n is my home;
And time's wild wintry blast
Soon shall be overpast;
I shall reach home at last,
Heav'n is my home.

There at my Savior's side
Heav'n is my home;
I shall be glorified,
Heav'n is my home.
There are the good and blest,
Those I love most and best;
And there I, too, shall rest,
Heav'n is my home.

Therefore I murmur not,
Heav'n is my home;
Whate'er my earthly lot,
Heav'n is my home;
And I shall surely stand
There at my Lord's right hand.
Heav'n is my fatherland,
Heav'n is my home.

Scripture Lessons for Next Sunday

Read in preparation for the Seventh Sunday of Easter
Acts 1:(1–7), 8–14; 1 Peter 4:12–17; 5:6–11; and John 17:1–11.

Session 16

The Seventh Sunday of Easter

Acts 1:(1–7), 8–14; 1 Peter 4:12–17; 5:6–11; John 17:1–11

Focus

Theme: *Suffering for the Sake of the Gospel*

Law/Gospel Focus

Because of our sinful nature, and because of the power of our spiritual enemies, we will at times suffer for the sake of the Gospel. God in Christ Jesus promises to protect us so that we can remain strong, firm, and steadfast until we receive the crown of eternal life.

Objectives

That by the power of the Holy Spirit working in us through God's Word we might
1. identify the sufferings that we, as Christians, may have to undergo for the sake of the Gospel;
2. identify the enemies of the Gospel that may seek to bring suffering into our lives because we are children of God through faith in Jesus Christ;
3. discover from the Scriptures the means that God has chosen to keep us firm in the faith even in the midst of suffering.

Opening Worship

Read responsively selected verses from Psalm 25.

Leader: To You, O LORD, I lift up my soul;

Participants: in You I trust, O my God. Do not let me be put to shame, nor let my enemies triumph over me.

Leader: No one whose hope is in You will ever be put to shame,

Participants: but they will be put to shame who are treacherous without excuse.

Leader: Show me Your ways, O L ORD , teach me Your paths;
Participants: guide me in Your truth and teach me, for You are
                     God my Savior, and my hope is in You all day
                     long.
Leader: Remember not the sins of my youth and my
                     rebellious ways;
Participants: according to Your love remember me, for You are
                     good, O L ORD .
Leader: Turn to me and be gracious to me,
Participants: for I am lonely and afflicted.
Leader: See how my enemies have increased and how
                     fiercely they hate me!
All: Guard my life and rescue me; let me not be put
                     to shame, for I take refuge in You.

   Join in singing "If You but Trust in God to Guide You," *LW* 420.

     If you but trust in God to guide you
     And place your confidence in Him,
     You'll find Him always there beside you
     To give you hope and strength within.
     For those who trust God's changeless love
     Build on the rock that will not move.

     What gain is there in futile weeping,
     In helpless anger and distress?
     If you are in His care and keeping,
     In sorrow will He love you less?
     For He who took for you a cross
     Will bring you safe through ev'ry loss.

     In patient trust await His leisure
     In cheerful hope, with heart content
     To take whate'er your Father's pleasure
     And all discerning love have sent;
     Doubt not your inmost wants are known
     To Him who chose you for His own.

     Sing, pray, and keep His ways unswerving,
     Offer your service faithfully,
     And trust His Word; though undeserving,

You'll find His promise true to be.
God never will forsake in need
The soul that trusts in Him indeed.

Introduction

Suffering occurs for many different reasons. Sometimes circumstances totally outside of our control bring us suffering. We may be driving carefully and within the speed limit down a familiar street when suddenly, out of nowhere a car comes crashing into us. Bones are broken and lives may be lost even though we had done nothing wrong.

But sometimes we bring suffering upon ourselves when we do things which are directly opposite to God's will for us revealed in the Bible. God's will for marriage is that one man and one woman make a commitment to each other for life. But many, including Christians, forsake their vows and give their love to another, bringing much heartache to themselves, their children, their families and their original partner.

Sometimes the devil uses the lure of money or sex or power to seduce men and women into living lives that are an affront to God and a danger to society. And so people suffer.

1. What suffering do people face because of sin in this world?

2. What suffering do people face because of their sins?

3. How can and/or does suffering affect our faith in Jesus?

The good news is that God has the prescription for lives that are filled with suffering, whether of our own making or as the result of other factors. And the main ingredient in that prescription is Jesus.

Inform

Read the summary of each of the Bible lessons appointed for the Seventh Sunday of Easter.

Acts 1:8–14—Jesus gave the promise of the power of the Holy Spirit and the command to be His witnesses everywhere. He then ascended into heaven, and the angels assured the disciples that He would one day return in the very same way that He had just left them.

The disciples returned to Jerusalem. Matthias is chosen as the disciple who will replace Judas. The disciples, the women, and Mary, the mother of Jesus, remain together in constant prayer as they await the promise of the outpouring of the Holy Spirit.

1 Peter 4:12–17; 5:6–11—Peter gives us a stark reminder of the cost of discipleship. Christians will be insulted on account of the name of Jesus and will face persecution and much suffering. But at the same time he promises that God will support us in our suffering and enable us to go through it without losing our faith. The key, Peter says, is to cast all our worries, cares and anxieties on God, and He will uplift us. He ends with a warning to be self-controlled and alert as the devil, like a roaring lion, prowls around seeking Christians to devour. Finally Peter gives us the words of assurance that God will in time restore us when suffering has run its course.

John 17:1–11—John records the words of Jesus as He prays for those He came to save. Jesus asks His Father to glorify Him now that the work of redemption might be complete. Jesus also prays for those He leaves behind as He prepares to leave this world and return to His Father in heaven.

1. Consider the life of the early Christian church. What are some of the sufferings that Christians endured for the sake of the Gospel?

2. Read 2 Corinthians 11:22–29. Write in the space below a list of the things that the apostle Paul suffered for the sake of the Gospel. Remember that this is only a partial listing. What astonishing words did Paul confess even after he reflected on the suffering he had endured? See 2 Corinthians 12:7–10, especially

verse 10. What enabled Paul to confess these words? See 2 Corinthians 12:9.

3. In 1 Peter 4:15–16, what does Peter say we are not to suffer for? Of what kind of suffering do we not need to be ashamed?

4. In 1 Peter 5:6–9 what five commands does Peter give us?

5. Who or what are some of the enemies that contemporary Christians must face today? Make a list.

6. What promises does God provide to us in 1 Peter 5:10; John 17:10–11; and 2 Corinthians 12:9? How do these promises enable you to face suffering with hope and confidence?

Connect

1. Read Romans 6:1–14 and Galatians 5:16–26. Like Peter, St. Paul urges us Christians to live in the spirit of God not following the ways of the world. Now look up Ephesians 6:10–20. What does

God provide for us to keep us strong in the faith even as we face suffering and hardships?

2. Can you think of a time in your life when suffering weighed you down? Share with the class, if you feel comfortable, the suffering that came into your life (physical, spiritual, and/or emotional) and how God enabled you to cope and to come through the suffering victorious and stronger in faith.

Vision

During This Week

1. Talk with family and friends about the enemies of God that seek to bring suffering that will cause us to turn away from God. Share the power that we have by faith in Christ to overcome all suffering.
2. Talk with your pastor. Ask if there is anyone for whom you can pray this week who is currently going through suffering in their life. Pray for that person.

Closing Worship

Read Psalm 23 together and end your time together today by praying The Lord's Prayer.

Scripture Lessons for Next Sunday

Read in preparation for the Day of Pentecost Joel 2:28–29; Acts 2:1–21; and John 16:5–11.

Session 17

The Day of Pentecost

Joel 2:28–29; Acts 2:1–21; John 16:5–11

Focus

Theme: *The Sound of the Spirit*

Law/Gospel Focus

People often hear the Word of God but refuse to listen. They miss out on the power of the Holy Spirit working through that Word to create saving faith. Despite this sinful inclination of our human nature to reject God, the Holy Spirit persistently endeavors to open the ears and hearts of people to Christ by implanting faith in hearts and minds through God's Word.

Objectives

That by the power of the Holy Spirit working in us through God's Word we might
1. hear the sounds of the Spirit speaking to us in the Scripture lessons appointed for the Day of Pentecost;
2. filter out the sounds of the world that would drown out God's Word to us and diminish the power of the Spirit working through that Word;
3. be empowered by the same Spirit who empowered the disciples on Pentecost so that we might fearlessly and faithfully speak the truth of the Gospel;
4. be enabled to see the result of the work of the Holy Spirit in us and in others and to praise God from whom all such blessings flow for His marvelous grace.

Opening Worship

Sing or speak together "Come Holy Ghost, God and Lord," *LW* 154.

Come Holy Ghost, God and Lord,
With all Your graces now outpoured
On each believer's mind and heart;
Your fervent love to them impart.
Lord, by the brightness of Your light
In holy faith Your Church unite;
From ev'ry land and ev'ry tongue
This to Your praise, O Lord, our God be sung:
Alleluia, alleluia!

Come, holy Light, guide divine,
Now cause the Word of life to shine.
Teach us to know our God aright
And call Him Father with delight.
From ev'ry error keep us free;
Let none but Christ our Master be
That we in living faith abide,
In Him, our Lord, with all our might confide.
Alleluia, alleluia!

Come, holy Fire, comfort true,
Grant us the will Your work to do
And in Your service to abide;
Let trials turn us not aside.
Lord, by Your pow'r prepare each heart,
And to our weakness strength impart
That bravely here we may contend,
Through life and death to You, our Lord, ascend.
Alleluia, alleluia!

Pray together:

Come, Holy Spirit, inspire our souls with the truth of Christ and His salvation for all people. Ignite our hearts to freely share the good news of God's love and forgiveness in Christ with all whom You lead us to encounter this week and throughout our lives.

Speak to us this day through the Scriptures we study together, so that through the words we hear we might grow in our love for God and our commitment to telling people about Jesus. This we ask of You, in His name. Amen.

Introduction

Technology today has enabled us to experience sound as never before. Many homes today are fully equipped with "surround sound" systems that make people feel "on location" as they watch a movie. Compact discs reproduce sound so faithfully that we are made to feel that we are in the concert hall.

Technology has also enabled us to filter out sounds that we do not want to hear. Our automobiles are now well-insulated for the quiet ride that is mandatory as we play our music in solitude. Laser technology has enabled us to filter out the background noises so common with records and early tapes.

Human beings also can filter out the sounds that we do not wish to hear. We have learned how to ignore them. We no longer listen to commercials on television. Children often choose to tune out their parents.

How sad it is, however, when people decide to tune out the Holy Spirit, who speaks today through God's Word, and refuse to believe what the Spirit says about Jesus as Savior. And how sad when Christians who have been redeemed by Christ and know it, refuse to listen to the prompting of the Spirit of God and listen instead to the sound and fury of the world.

1. What causes people to tune out the Word of God and, in so doing, the Holy Spirit's faith-creating and -strengthening power?

2. What might we do to eliminate those things that may cause us to tune out the Word of God? others to tune out the Word of God?

Inform

Read the summary of the lessons for the Day of Pentecost.

Joel 2:28–29—God promises through the prophet Joel that one day He will pour out His Spirit upon all His people. Then people will prophecy and dream dreams and see visions. God promises to pour out His Spirit upon men and women, young and old, who are His servants.

Acts 2:1–21—The disciples were all gathered together in one place and suddenly a sound like a violent wind swept through the house and what seemed to be tongues of fire appeared on the heads of the disciples. They began to speak in different languages. People from all over the world had gathered together in Jerusalem, and every person heard the disciples speaking in their own language, declaring the wonders of God. Peter explained to the crowd that they were witnessing the fulfillment of Joel's prophecy that God would pour out His Spirit upon His people.

John 16:5–11—Jesus tells the disciples that He is leaving them and that the Counselor, the Holy Spirit, would come in fulfillment of God's prophecy. The task of the Holy Spirit, according to Jesus, is to expose the guilt of people in regard to sin, righteousness, and judgment.

1. Describe in your own words the scene described in Acts 2:1–4.

2. What did Jesus promise in our Gospel Lesson?

3. The "Sounds of the Past": What had God, through the prophet Joel, promised hundreds of years before the Pentecost event?

4. "The Sounds of Pentecost": How do you think the disciples reacted when they heard the roaring of wind but felt no wind? saw the tongues of fire on their heads? spoke languages they had never learned?

5. What change was immediately evident in the disciples?

6. According to Acts 2:15 what did the people who witnessed this outpouring of the Holy Spirit think?

7. What is Peter's explanation for all of this?

8. Reread the Gospel Lesson. Then read the words that follow— John 16:12–15. Why does Jesus call the Holy Spirit, "the Counselor"?

Connect

1. Pentecost was the fulfillment of Joel's prophecy. The Holy Spirit was poured out upon His servants and wonderful things happened. How do we today receive the gift of the Holy Spirit? See Acts 2:38–39; and 10:44–48.

2. Next to each of the following Bible passages write the particular task or function of the Holy Spirit indicated.
   a. 1 Corinthians 6:11
   b. 1 Corinthians 12:3
   c. 2 Thessalonians 2:14

d. John 3:5–6
e. 1 Peter 1:23
f. Romans 8:9
g. Galatians 5:22–23
h. Philippians 1:6

3. According to Acts 7:51, why don't some people believe in Jesus as their Savior?

4. The Holy Spirit speaks today through the sounds of Baptism, the sounds of God's Word proclaimed and read, and the sounds of the Lord's Supper. Why is it important for you as a child of God by faith to be in God's Word regularly, remember daily your Baptism, and receive often the Sacrament of the Altar?

5. How has the Holy Spirit, working through God's Word and Sacrament, enabled you to filter out the sounds of the world that might distract you or lead you away from hearing God and His desire for your life?

Vision

During This Week

1. Find your Baptism certificate. Place it in a conspicuous place and every morning when you arise, look at it and say a prayer of thanks to God that He gave you the Holy Spirit and faith through Holy Baptism.
2. If you have children, sit down with them, show them their Baptism certificates. Share with them the importance of their baptism and how the Holy Spirit brought them to faith.

3. Write a prayer of thanks to the Holy Spirit for bringing you to faith and for continuing to strengthen you and keep you in your faith in Jesus.

Closing Worship

Close with the singing of "Holy Spirit, Light Divine," *LW* 166.

> Holy Spirit, light divine,
> Dawn upon this soul of mine;
> Let Your Word dispel the night,
> Wake my spirit, clear my sight.
>
> Holy Spirit, grace divine,
> Cleanse this sinful heart of mine;
> In Your mercy look on me,
> From sin's bondage set me free.
>
> Holy Spirit, truth divine,
> Shine upon these eyes of mine;
> Send Your radiance from above,
> Let me know my Savior's love.
>
> Holy Spirit, pow'r divine,
> Fortify this will of mine;
> Bend it to Your own pure will,
> All my life with graces fill.
>
> Holy Spirit, peace divine,
> Still this restless heart of mine;
> Speak to calm the tossing sea,
> Stayed in Your tranquility.
>
> Holy Spirit, all divine,
> Dwell within this self of mine;
> I Your temple pure would be
> Now and for eternity.

Scripture Lessons for Next Sunday

Read in preparation for the Holy Trinity Deuteronomy 4:32–34, 39–40; 2 Corinthians 13:11–14; and Matthew 28:16–20.